People Suck, God Is Good

PRAISE FOR PEOPLE SUCK, GOD IS GOOD

Dr. Walls has done a great job of confronting the biggest issue preventing genuine Christian unity- us! We clamor for peace and complain about brokenness while underestimating our contributions to the problem. This book is an honest and heartfelt journey toward genuine Christian unity in a "Third Space." -Rev. Dr. Jeff Philpott, Senior Pastor, Sandhills Community Church

People Suck, God is Good is a must-read! Malcolm Walls is authentic, the real deal, and honest about his upbringing and how God has changed his worldview. Malcolm tried to control the narrative, and in the end, his eyes were opened to a whole new way of seeing life. I encourage you to read this book; it could change your life. -Dr. David Olshine, Director and Professor of Youth Ministry, Family, and Culture at Columbia International University, Author of *The Mystery of Silence: Making Sense of life When God seems Absent*

This book exposes and examines the basic struggle Christians have in their daily walk to be more like Jesus. Dr. Walls accomplished a masterful combination of realness with academia in this book. People can walk away with a deeper understanding and a desire to fulfill a call to action. -Sala Funderburgh, Fortune 500 Company, Senior Manager

Dr. Walls does an excellent job of being transparent & vulnerable without compromising his authenticity and leaving you reminded this isn't a race issue; it's a faith issue. Reader, you need to be ready to laugh, cry, get ruffled, and be motivated to get catalytic for the changes needed to glorify God in your walk with Jesus. -Stephen Splawn, Pastor of First Northeast Baptist, Columbia, SC

This book shares Dr. Walls' vulnerability and honesty in a way that challenges the reader to consider their journey. He has a beautiful way of making the reader recognize their own bias to help them strive towards healing individually and as a community to have unity in the church. Great read!! -Pastor Tiffany S. Murphy, Dmin '16, Pemberton UMC, Pemberton, NJ

Listen up, Rev. Dr. Malcolm Walls has poured out his soul in these pages to wake us up! Despite the division and racial prejudice that persists, God is using him to stir our hearts toward unity in the church. Don't sleep on this word from my long-time friend in the struggle! -Drew G. I. Hart, Associate Professor of Theology at Messiah University and Author of Who Will Be A Witness: Igniting Activism for God's Justice, Love, and Deliverance

Dr. Malcolm Walls is a refreshing voice that is needed in the church. His transparency and brutal honesty about life, ministry, and God's love is going to bless everyone who reads this book. -Dr. Michael K Heath, Pastor, Campbell AME Church, Philadelphia, and US Army Chaplain

If you enter the reading of this book with a posture of learning, you just may discover how past experiences have cemented self-limiting beliefs about yourself which are holding you back from all that God would have you be. If you are open to reflection on Dr. Walls' journey, you will come away with heart change in yourself and a renewed hope for unity in the church. -Pamela J. Smith, Executive Leadership Coach

In our current age of tribalism, immediate outrage, and a default to divide, Pastor Malcolm Walls brings to light our desperate need as followers of the Way to pause, reflect on our own distortions, and seek the Holy Spirit's power to align our dissonances to Christ. With compelling narratives of his own struggles and victories, Pastor Walls reminds us all that seeking unity on common ground, in love, is our call and witness to a broken world. This is a poignant message that is needed for this current generation and for those to come. As you read, may this message be planted on fertile soil and yield a harvest one hundredfold. -J.H. Kim, Founder of Spark the Solution, LLC Private Equity Group

Pastor Malcolm brings a refreshing, honest, and raw take on how badly we need to examine ourselves and figure out what role we play in God's kingdom. Are we uniting or dividing it? He opens up your eyes to biblical truths on how we might be hurting the kingdom because of personal biases and past experiences, but also how God has provided the answers in his word to overcome and become the Dream Team representing the kingdom of God. -Pastor Elismar Rodriguez, Legacy Faith Church, Harrisburg, PA

Dr. Walls courageously and openly discusses things only talked about in private spaces and behind closed doors. He shows a self-awareness and personal vulnerability that forces the reader to examine their own hearts and spiritual formations. I immediately had to pause and pray for the Lord to examine my mind and my heart so the revelation could lead to repentance and a renewed spirit within me. -Dr. Larry L Anderson Jr., Author of *The Pastors' Diaries* and Co-Author of *Ask Me Why I'm Not In Church: A Call for the Church to Get Out of the Building*

People Suck, God Is Good

Breaking down walls, building toward unity

Dr. Malcolm Walls, Jr.

SMS MINISTRIES

Copyright © 2024 by Dr. Malcolm Walls, Jr.

Printed in the United States of America. All rights reserved. Written permission must be secured from the publisher to use or reproduce any part of this book, except for brief quotations in critical reviews or articles.

Published by SMS Ministries in Killeen, Texas. First Printing, 2024

SMS Ministries books may be purchased in bulk for educational, business, fundraising, or sales promotional use. For information about please email publishing@SMSMinistries.co.

Unless otherwise noted, all Scripture quotations are taken from the English Standard version ®, Copyright © 1999, 2000, 2002, 2003, 2009 by Holman Bible Publishers. Used by permission. Holman Christian Standard Bible®, Holman CSB®, and HCSB® are federally registered trademarks of Holman Bible Publishers.

Scripture quotations marked (NCV) are taken from the New Century Version®. Copyright © 2005 by Thomas Nelson. Used by permission. All rights reserved.

Scripture quotations marked (NIV) are taken from the Holy Bible, New International Version. Copyright © 1973, 1978, 1984 by the International Bible Society. Used by permission of the International Bible Society.

ISBN: 978-1-7350847-6-3

I want to thank my Lord and Savior, Jesus Christ, for allowing me to pursue writing this book and sharing it with others. Thank you, Lord, for the journey I have been on and how you have given me countless opportunities to engage with people different than myself. All those experiences have helped me to be better and love people like You love them.

I want to thank my wife, Tiffanie, for her continuous encouragement and wisdom to help me be a better husband, father, and pastor. Your motivation through this whole process has been invaluable. I love you, and thank you for never giving up on me, always loving me, and relentlessly pushing me to be the best I can be.

I also want to thank my children, Imani, Malcolm, and Alex. You all keep me laughing and inspire me to strive to be my best. There is greatness in each of you. Tap into it and continue to be better.

I want to thank my mom. You are a fighter, and your testimony has taught me never to give up.

I want to thank my sister, Sala, and my brother, Wes. Our conversations are priceless; your collective wisdom, humor, and perspective on life have educated me and helped me get through some tough times.

Lastly, to my father, you could have started your race better...but you finished strong. I love you!

CONTENTS

PRAISE FOR PEOPLE SUCK, GOD IS GOOD — ii
DEDICATION — vii

Foreword — 1

Introduction — 3

1. Fighting the Wrong Enemy — 7
2. Echoes from the Past — 18
3. People Suck — 29
4. The Monster in the Mirror — 43
5. Focused on God's Glory — 61
6. Operating in God's Space — 86
7. Faith in Action: Three Little E's — 94
8. Loving People God's Way — 106
9. Eyes of Grace — 123
10. All Words Matter — 136

CONTENTS

11 | One Sound, One Heart 150

12 | God is Good: An Invitation 159

ACKNOWLEDGEMENTS 165
ABOUT THE AUTHOR 166
REFERENCES 167

Foreword

I couldn't be more honored to write the foreword for this book. Rev. Dr. Malcolm Walls, or Malcolm, as I refer to him, is a great friend and fellow pastor. We have been on very different, yet strangely similar, journeys for many years. God brought our paths together nearly six years ago. We have been learning together how the Great Commandment of "loving God and loving others" works in real life.

In this book, with its reality-based title, Dr. Walls is candidly transparent. My brother invites us into his private journey with surprising candor. (I learned several new things about my friend.) With his leadership, we explore the truth of scripture, the pain of brokenness, and the promise of what Christ offers. In the end, we are offered a picture of what Christ-honoring relationships can be.

Brokenness is real in all its varied forms. When our brokenness interacts with the brokenness of the world around us, sin isn't far behind. When you add to this a supernatural, unseen enemy, our situation is ripe for disaster. We see the effects in our world every day: shattered lives and relationships, ethnic and economic discrimination, brutality, betrayal, and all the many versions of sin that mankind can invent to hurt one another.

Dr. Walls doesn't just want to point out the reality of a broken world or even the ideal that God offers us through Christ. He wants to confront the very real, unseen struggle within each of us. He asks powerful and insightful questions to probe the depths of depravity in ourselves and the world. This journey toward wholeness is painful.

However, with the help of our Lord, there is hope. And best of all, God is glorified!

As humanity, we are an insecure version of what we should have been before our historic fall. So, we are always looking for ways to elevate ourselves. The primary way we do this is by looking for ways to put others down — to consider ourselves superior to them in whatever manner, from economic prosperity to skin color, from national origin to sports teams.

Dr. Walls and I have been fortunate to teach a class together at Columbia Biblical Seminary focused on multiethnic ministry. Except for all the grading, it has been a sincere joy to do this with my brother. One of the things we teach our students is the difference between being "open to" and "intentional toward." Almost everyone and every church is "open to" relationships with people different from themselves. However, very few are "intentional toward" developing those relationships or making a place for them in our church. We are hesitant to pursue these relationships because our differences make it messy. The beauty is not denying differences but acknowledging them, embracing them, and even celebrating them. We all need friends who don't look like us, think like us, or vote like us.

Dr. Walls and I, by God's grace, have stepped together into a "Third Space" as peacemakers. Care to join us?

Dr. Jeff Philpott
Lead Pastor, Sandhills Community Church

Introduction

> *The entire agenda of the enemy can be boiled down to one objective: embarrass God through some of His children.* - **A.W. Tozer**

In my 40-plus years of living, I have come to learn that we all, regardless of skin color, gender, theology, or economic class, have the propensity to be sucky people. We all fall short of God's holy standard. To some degree, we are all prideful, and because we are so self-absorbed, we rarely consider the possibility that we are the problem. Even when we enter into a relationship with Jesus, the lack of self-awareness (related to our sins, blind spots, and past struggles) impacts our relationships with others, especially our brothers and sisters in Christ.

I have learned that people tend to leave or avoid the church altogether because of *how people act*, not because of *who God is*. In all my years of ministry, I have never had someone leave the church because "God looked at me with a side-eye when I came in." From my experience as a pastor, God has repeatedly shown me that you and I often contribute to the disunity and lack of peace with others, specifically those in the church. I have also learned that even when we seek to be the best versions of ourselves, we still allow our sins to influence how we act, think, and view others.

It is incredible how past trauma and our environments growing up have shaped and impacted the way we think. Perhaps you are reading this book and have a negative view of the opposite sex or other ethnic groups because of your negative personal experiences. Maybe you are holding on to a past betrayal and projecting it on others. No matter what it is, we all have biases and baggage that we carry around, allowing it to shape us and the way we interact with others.

If you find it difficult to have unity and be at peace with others, welcome to the club. I am a black Christian man who still gets upset when I see that someone who looks like me is killed or mistreated by the police without just cause. I am a black Christian who often lives with internal conflict regarding how people with brown skin are treated worldwide. I still get offended at jokes that even remotely sound like they are about black people. Sometimes, it is hard for me to love others who do not share my way of thinking or who struggle with sins different from mine. Sometimes, I realize that I also have unconscious biases about other issues. In light of all this (or perhaps despite all this), I am writing this book because I genuinely believe that even with all our differences, biases, and baggage, there is a way forward, and unity can be obtained.

The truth is that we all struggle to love those who are different from us. This should come as no surprise because Ephesians 2 reminds us that as believers, we all, at some point, have followed the course of this world. Part of the course of this world is disregarding people from other cultures and their experiences. We often ignore those who struggle with mental illness. We treat inmates, ex-offenders, and immigrants as if they don't exist. We are imperfect people, so we should not be shocked that division exists in the universal church — we bring it in! For followers of Christ to hold onto narrow views of thinking and embrace ideologies toxic to the faith brings dishonor to the Lord and goes against our new nature in Christ. Instead of letting the old nature die, there are moments when we resurrect it, embrace the old mindset, and live in a way where grace and unconditional love no longer bind us together in the body of Christ.

In the high priestly prayer in John 17, Jesus starts by praying for glory. In John 17:1, Jesus prayed for himself to be glorified so that he would glorify the Father. God's glory is the foundational focus of the

PEOPLE SUCK, GOD IS GOOD

prayer. He then prays for the disciples. He prays that they would be sanctified and kept safe in the world. After that, he prays for all those who will believe. This is the church. You and me. Jesus prays for unity in love, truth, and mission among his disciples because when we walk in harmony, it brings glory to the Father and proclaims the magnificence of God to the world.

In that prayer and at the moment before Jesus is about to be arrested, when it came to us, the church, He could have prayed for anything first. He could have prayed for our holiness or justice around the world. He could have prayed to end poverty or for every church building to be a beautiful place with great programs. He could have prayed that we would have an easy life without unnecessary drama. He could have prayed that we would all be healthy. But he doesn't pray for any of that. In John 17:21, the first thing he prayed for was our oneness. Jesus mentions the word "one" related to unity among believers four times in verses 20-26. Oneness is crucial for followers of Jesus because He knows the power that unity brings and how easy it is for us to become divided.

With a pastoral heart and sincere prayer, I hope this book will provoke you to go before God so that He can show you who you are in Christ, change any worldly thinking you may have, and help you overcome any strongholds that hinder our oneness in Christ. As I continue to fight my battles, I have learned that many believers want peace in the church. We want to experience the kingdom of God and His *shalom*, or peace, among His children. But our fight for oneness is no easy task. The attack on the church to keep us from being one has not stopped and will never stop until we die or Jesus comes back. But as believers, no matter what, we are called to fight. 2 Corinthians 10:3-5 says,

> [3] For though we walk in the flesh, we are not waging war according to the flesh. [4] For the weapons of our warfare are not of the flesh but have divine power to destroy strongholds. [5] We destroy arguments and every lofty opinion raised against the knowledge of God and take every thought captive to obey Christ.

In the call to fight, we are fighting against our greatest enemy... ourselves! We are fighting to deny ourselves and surrender to the Lordship of Christ daily.

One of my motives for writing this book is to help facilitate conversations where we uncover our blindspots, recognize how we contribute to the problem, embrace our differences, and leverage those differences to advance the kingdom of God. If we are going to accomplish true unity, we must all come to the table and combat the sins that so easily beset us. It must begin by submitting our minds to God and allowing Him to destroy the strongholds that hinder us from moving forward.

While reading, I pray that this book challenges you to find and create pathways that seek unity with others despite the discomfort that will inevitably be felt. I am tired of seeing the church divided. However, I am confident that as we keep fighting, we will indeed come together and be extensions of divine oneness for the glory of God and live out Revelation 7:9.

> After this I looked, and behold, a great multitude that no one could number, from every nation, from all tribes and peoples and languages, standing before the throne and before the Lamb, clothed in white robes, with palm branches in their hands, and crying out with a loud voice, "Salvation belongs to our God who sits on the throne, and to the Lamb!"

1

Fighting the Wrong Enemy

> *For we do not wrestle against flesh and blood...*
> — **Ephesians 6:12**

In the movie *Rocky V*, Rocky Balboa retires because of the damage he suffered from fighting Ivan Drago. He then spirals into a financial crisis. To make a financial comeback, he takes a young boxer, Tommy Gunn, under his wings and begins to train him. Tommy becomes more successful as time passes and is being compared to Rocky. He wants to climb the championship ranks quickly, but Rocky advises Tommy to take it slow. Ignoring Rocky's advice and wanting to step out of his shadow, Tommy is lured away from Rocky and partners with the antagonist boxing promoter, George Washington Duke, who cunningly promises Tommy more money and a shot at the heavyweight title. With Duke by his side, Tommy's relationship with Rocky is broken, and he becomes the heavyweight boxing champ.

However, Tommy is not respected in the boxing world and is still in Rocky's shadow. In Tommy's mind, to gain respect, he has to fight and beat the one who helped him start his boxing career. SPOILER ALERT: At the end of the movie, Rocky and Tommy, who once had a great relationship, begin squaring off in a street fight. As they fight, Tommy takes the upper hand and starts destroying Rocky. Punch after punch, it seems like Rocky is destined to lose. While being pummeled, Rocky has flashbacks of other fights where he has been viciously beaten. Then Rocky hears the voice of his former trainer, Mickey, who says, "I didn't hear no bell! Get up!" Rocky gets up and, in classic Rocky fashion, defeats Tommy.

Unfortunately, I have seen similar scenes play out in the lives of Jesus followers. With their new life in Christ, they find themselves in crisis, and then they find a lifeline. They befriend other believers, join a new church, and life starts going well. They find healing and hope in these new relationships, but something happens. A presidential election, police shooting, pandemic, protest, riot, a pastor says something controversial, and just like that, they are now fighting each other over those things. A peaceful and respectful relationship is in jeopardy, like Tommy and Rocky, because they have different perspectives.

Brothers and sisters who have good intentions in the Christian faith are now fighting one another about social injustice, vaccines, ethnic oppression, politics, theology, and economics. And as verbal punches (and maybe some literal punches) are thrown, it leads to feelings of hurt, betrayal, frustration, anger, and confusion. Wait, where is the antagonist Duke, the outside instigator? Outside instigators can come in many forms, including the media, politicians, rallies, movements, voices of influencers, and various social media posts that seek our full attention. Satan uses all of these instigators, and his goal is to destroy godly relationships. His motives are purely selfish. And with instigators arresting people's attention in the church, instead of living in peaceful relationships with one another, we live in division where people are labeled based on the color of their skin, political affiliation, socioeconomic class, theology, or cultural background.

How do I know all of this? Unfortunately, I have lived it. I have lost friendships due to my immaturity and selfishness. On one occasion, like Rocky versus Tommy Gunn, I recall being in a parking lot about to fight a pastor with whom I had been friends with for over eight years. Before this moment, we shared our struggles and victories. Our families were close. We had a great relationship. But at the end of the eight years, we argued because we did not see eye to eye on a particular issue. He wanted things his way, and I wanted them my way. And all of a sudden, an argument almost turned into a street brawl. There we were, two pastors in a parking lot in North Philadelphia at night, about to fight because we could not civilly agree to disagree. But this is one example of how issues have divided people. Let's recap some events that have created issues between people and ushered in more division within the church.

In 2020, we experienced racial tension, protests, riots, financial stress, police hostility, political polarization, gender identity arguments, and a pandemic. As we moved into 2021, we saw more changes. We got a new commander-in-chief. Two new Covid-19 variants surfaced. White men were introduced to the black experience of being labeled a threat. They endured being called toxic, homophobic, privileged, and racist simply because they were white.

In 2022, we heard things like, "You can't be a Christian and vote Democrat." The monkeypox virus began to spread, Russia invaded Ukraine, and the Supreme Court overturned the *Roe v. Wade* decision on abortion. In 2023, the Supreme Court ended affirmative action for colleges, declaring race cannot be a factor when admitting students. And with all that going on, the church moved along with the culture and became puppets to media and politics.

The pulpit on Sunday was used to preach and promote personal ideologies, feelings about political leaders, liberalism, conservatism, masks, etc. For every step we took forward to create unity in the church, we seemed to take two steps back when something controversial happened in the world. Unity had become a forgotten virtue, and what kingdom benefit has come from a divided church? Here is my list of answers, but please feel free to make your list.

1. None.

Division in the church reflects what we see in the world. In divided churches, there is finger-pointing and passive aggression where no one takes ownership of the madness. Division among churches has led to some churches falling into the sin of thinking they "do church" better than others. Some reformed churches think charismatic churches are too emotional, and charismatic churches think reformed churches are too academic. There is also a lack of interculturalism in churches, further promoting segregation. All of this reinforces that one group is superior to another. Aren't we tired of the division? From a kingdom perspective, there can be distinction among churches, but there should not be division unless unrepentant sin or heresy is involved.

As a pastor, I have had the privilege of speaking and engaging with various groups of Christians. In one group, it was evident that they had grown weary and disheartened by the hateful rhetoric and actions that were going on in the free world and how it had spilled over into the church. These individuals had invested portions of their lives being peacemakers in the church. As they thought about the biblical mandate for the people of God to live as one, they became vexed by what they saw in their church and what they read on social media from other brothers and sisters in the faith.

Some Christians felt that there was no point fighting for peace and unity of any sort. Still, others chose to leave the local church altogether and opt for online worship so they would not have to interact with people. In 2020, many families and friendships were fractured because of offenses, emotionalism, and differing views on race, gender, policing, and politics. As I looked at my Facebook feed, I saw people who love Jesus waving the proverbial white flag because of posts made by fellow Christians. Christians, both liberal and conservative, were publicly attacking each other on various topics, and it seemed as if the truth of scripture was no longer the deciding factor in how we engaged with each other.

As Christians, we allowed the culture to fill us with lies that our enemies were inherently Republican or Democrat, gay or straight, rich or poor, Baptist or Presbyterian, black, brown or white. And as we absorbed all that the culture offered, it left us, the church, more vulnerable to believe the lies being thrown at us. Not only did we become distracted by the things of the world, but we also were in our feelings, lashing out at one another and justifying it by sprinkling a little scripture on it.

As all this happened, some of us stood by and watched the carnage, wondering, "Aren't we better than this?" I was reminded of a sermon from Dr. Martin Luther King Jr., who shared how America had advanced scientifically and technologically but struggled to advance morally and spiritually.

I also talked to some very spirited, well-intentioned Christians who were passionate about our country's current moral and spiritual standing. They fiercely proclaimed that America was a Christian country with Christian values and were mad if someone disagreed with their position. They spoke as if America had no sin, making it divine while ignoring the divisiveness that exists. I talked to other well-intentioned Christians who were hoping the government could fix all our problems. Some individuals have connected themselves to social movements and subscribed to the feeling that the "haves" must give to the "have-nots." I also spoke with believers who have continued to travel down the rabbit hole of secularism. They have allowed their compassion about gender, abortion, and other hot-button issues to dilute the scriptures. As a result, at the expense of the truth of God's word, they have embraced secular culture and canceled friendships with others that had kingdom value. Pastor and author Dane Ortlund wrote:

> ...if we allow the world around us in our present cultural moment to dictate to us the significance of friendship, we not only lose out on a reality vital to human flourishing at the horizontal level; we lose out, even worse, on enjoying the friendship of Christ at a vertical level.[1]

I also met with Christians who had become pharisaical by mandating that others assimilate to their personal opinions and beliefs, yet their ethics did not match their doctrine. They allowed their sociology to dictate their theology, which led to them embracing a Jesus that is not the Jesus of the Bible but an emotional, situational, and circumstantial Jesus based on legalism and personal opinions.

One of the most disturbing observations I have made so far is that Christians have begun to question the salvation of other Christians because of how they are politically and socially aligned. Could it be that we have forgotten, as believers, that our fight is not against flesh and blood? We preach and teach it, but somehow, due to "spiritual amnesia," we have started holding friends and acquaintances at arm's length. We treat them as if they are the enemy when they are not.

Since unity is the will of God, we must conclude that Satan desires to divide the people of God. He is the enemy, and 1 Peter 5:8-9 reminds us who we are against. "Be sober-minded; be watchful. Your adversary, the devil prowls around like a roaring lion, seeking someone to devour. Resist him, firm in your faith, knowing that the same kinds of suffering are being experienced by your brotherhood throughout the world."

In his New Testament Commentary, author and Bible teacher Warren Wiersbe wrote:

> Satan is a dangerous enemy. He is a serpent who can bite when we least expect it. He is a destroyer... He has great power and intelligence and a host of demons who assist him in his attacks against God's people...[2]

Pastor John MacArthur wrote:

> He (Satan) and his forces are always active, looking for opportunities to overwhelm the believer with temptation, persecution, and discouragement. Satan sows discord with his accusations to God

> about men, men about God, and men about men. He will do what he can to drag the Christian out of fellowship with Christ and out of Christian service.[3]

Satan is indeed working. As followers of Christ, he has duped us into thinking our battle is against each other. We have become theologically disoriented, socially destitute, and emotionally distracted. Could it be that we have gotten so caught up in our religion that we have neglected our relationship with God and one another?

There is another ugly truth. We are also fighting our very own flesh. Remember, I was in a parking lot about to fight another pastor. This could have been a YouTube moment. He and I have discussed that altercation since then and agreed that our selfishness led to that moment. The enemy would have loved it if we had come to blows that evening. He would have enjoyed it if we would have let our flesh win. Praise God that a friend of mine was there to keep us from embarrassing ourselves, our families, and our churches. We must ask ourselves, "Do we want to keep fighting each other and continue in division? Or do we want to fight our flesh and against the enemy for unity? Other questions we need to ask ourselves are, "Have we gotten too comfortable with our flesh and forgotten that we are in a spiritual war? Can we have enough self-awareness to recognize that we all are equally human, equally broken, and have blind spots? After deciding to follow Jesus, we must be aware that we are being progressively sanctified to truly live out the oneness God calls us to live out with other believers. Considering this should compel us as children of God to intentionally fight for oneness in the body of Christ and die to our flesh. We should want to do this if for nothing else, to demonstrate the power of the Gospel to those who do not believe. I believe many people in the faith are tired of dealing with all the divisiveness. Some have reached the peak of frustration and claim that change is impossible. Others are in the "sick-and-tired" camp and are experiencing fatigue on high levels. They are experiencing racial, political, social, and theological fatigue coupled with the fatigue of their struggles with sin. But I believe that Jesus is telling us, like Mickey told Rocky, "I didn't hear no bell! Get up!" So, let's get up and go one more round!

I have spent years running from racism, classism, sexism, and other -isms because of my traumatic experiences. But somehow, in my running, I have found myself serving in a multi-ethnic, multicultural, diverse socioeconomic and loving, yet still broken, church in Columbia, South Carolina, and teaching and speaking on ethnic unification and peacemaking. I have been tempted to think that things will never get better. I have been tempted to have more parking lot moments. I have been labeled a liberal and perhaps even a conservative sell-out by some. Yet, God has led me to a point in my life where I am compelled to push forward — compelled to love, journey, unify, and make peace. I have decided to fight as God's ambassador because that is what love demands. The idea of unity goes against the individualistic culture we are bombarded with daily. Like any other sin, I have realized that the issues that divide us don't just die; we must put them to death. Colossians 3:5-17 says:

> "[5] Put to death therefore what is earthly in you: sexual immorality, impurity, passion, evil desire, and covetousness, which is idolatry. [6] On account of these the wrath of God is coming. [7] In these you too once walked, when you were living in them. [8] But now you must put them all away: anger, wrath, malice, slander, and obscene talk from your mouth. [9] Do not lie to one another, seeing that you have put off the old self with its practices [10] and have put on the new self, which is being renewed in knowledge after the image of its creator. [11] Here there is not Greek and Jew, circumcised and uncircumcised, barbarian, Scythian, slave, free; but Christ is all, and in all. [12] Put on then, as God's chosen ones, holy and beloved, compassionate hearts, kindness, humility, meekness, and patience, [13] bearing with one another and, if one has a complaint against another, forgiving each other; as the Lord has forgiven you, so you also must forgive. [14] And above all these put

on love, which binds everything together in perfect harmony. ¹⁵ And let the peace of Christ rule in your hearts, to which indeed you were called in one body. And be thankful. ¹⁶ Let the word of Christ dwell in you richly, teaching and admonishing one another in all wisdom, singing psalms and hymns and spiritual songs, with thankfulness in your hearts to God. ¹⁷ And whatever you do, in word or deed, do everything in the name of the Lord Jesus, giving thanks to God the Father through him."

In the scripture above, there is a call to put to death *and* a call to put on life. It is a one-two punch. If we are going to put something to death, that means it is alive. Anything that is living will fight to stay alive. We must fight to kill the things that divide us, ultimately leading to feelings of pain, misunderstanding, fear, mistreatment, oppression, hopelessness, and worthlessness. But we must still fight to kill the sins that stem from evil desires, selfishness, and pride.

The things that divide us will not relinquish their hold on those in the body of Christ or those in the world. Neither will the anger and pain of those affected let go to allow people to experience healing. We must roll up our sleeves, look in the mirror, fight against our sinful nature, and be vigilant to create unity with others and live out the prayer of Jesus in John 17:21, "...that they may all be one, just as you, Father, are in me, and I in you, that they also may be in us, so that the world may believe that you have sent me." We will explore John 17 more throughout the book. Still, as you can see, the byproduct of the unified church is tremendous. We are not just fighting for peace and unification but also glorification. The more we fight for oneness, the more unity exists, and the more Jesus can be seen in the world, allowing people to believe. And when they believe, God gets more glory.

The church should be the gold standard for how people interact. But when the church is no longer the solution or makes halfhearted attempts at oneness without any sacrifice, we become part of the problem. We must reevaluate if our hearts and actions are in step with scripture. We have made progress, but God calls us to live out our faith as one in Christ. John explains it in 1 John 4:20-21 when he writes:

> "If anyone says, "I love God," and hates his brother, he is a liar; for he who does not love his brother whom he has seen cannot love God whom he has not seen. And this commandment we have from him: whoever loves God must also love his brother."

Truly loving each other is an arduous, but not impossible, task. The crux of unification is to join together things that are opposed to each other from the outset. Just like a marriage, you have two different people, with all of their quirks, coming together and making a covenant to be one. It is a process of growing together and understanding that you are both equal. If one spouse thinks they are superior to the other, serious conflict is inevitable. Unity takes time and can be messy, but when done with the power of God, it is well worth it. Mark Deymaz, author and pastor of a multi-ethnic and economically diverse church, said it best when he wrote:

> So Jews were loving Gentiles, Gentiles were loving Jews, and they were all worshiping God together as one in the local church at Antioch. Yes, it blew everyone away! This was unprecedented, remarkable, amazing, and miraculous, for only a Prince of Peace can bring peace to historically estranged people groups; only a Messiah can unite the world as one by sowing love into the hearts of those who for so long had been filled with hate.[4]

To eradicate division in the church, we must understand all the mess that we carry and not let that impact relationships. In hindsight, that night in the parking lot in North Philadelphia, I brought pride, burnout, and stress to the argument. However, in that heated moment, I wasn't aware of all I was dealing with emotionally. And for others, they are often unaware of their emotions and struggles. We are unaware that we still carry a history of abuse, immorality, injustice, broken homes, oppression, violence, pain, anger, discontent, personal disappointment, etc. Unification does not discount one's past or current reality; however, it does seek to move forward without continuously rehashing a record of wrongs or living in a perpetual state of discontent with others. We have to, somehow, be aware of the baggage we are carrying but not let it dictate how we engage with people.

The church has been divided for way too long, and as disciples of Jesus, destroying it begins with us. As you read about some of my journey in the following chapters, you will find practical ways to shatter the walls that divide us and insight into how God uses the power of forgiveness, the beauty of confession, and the strength of love to create unity with others.

2

Echoes from the Past

> *Remember not the former things, nor consider the things of old.* — Isaiah 43:18

Today, I strive to love all people, and the Lord has burdened my heart to have compassion on everyone. But I was not always like this. Over the course of my life, I've learned a lot of lessons. I learned to become a racist person, was the victim of racism, distrusted anyone who was white, and objectified women. If you had asked me over 20 years ago if I was racist or hedonistic, I would have told you "No," but in my mind, I would say to myself, "Absolutely." At one point in my life, white people were the devil and women were simply a means to an end. This is what I was taught and, subsequently, what I believed. But how did it all start? And more importantly, how did it all change?

I grew up in Greenville, Mississippi, also known as the Delta. I remember enjoying things like fishing, roller skating on Friday nights, swimming at the local community pool across from Greenville High School, listening to good music, and eating freshly fried catfish with hot sauce and Wonder Bread. My father often took me to the Delta Blues Festival, where I gained a genuine appreciation for the blues. My dad went out of his way to have me listen to music by artists like Muddy Waters and B.B. King. I even had the opportunity to meet Ralph Macchio, Joe Seneca, and other cast members of the 1986 movie *Crossroads*.

My mom and dad also introduced me to black professionals and the best of southern black culture. Through them and my older sister, I met and mingled with lawyers, doctors, entrepreneurs, mechanics, educators, and entertainers. We went to St. Matthews A.M.E. (African Methodist Episcopal) Church in Greenville, which was a predominantly black church in a black neighborhood. I also fell in love with Historically Black Colleges because of my parents. Overall, I had a well-rounded, black-centered southern childhood.

I was the only boy on my mom's side of the family. One of my aunts was a teacher, and the others were nurses. It was always good to see them because they would spoil me rotten. When I was with them, they were very protective of me. When my mom and aunts talked among themselves and thought no one was listening, I got to hear how they viewed the world. I learned a few things from them:

> Lesson #1 - Black folks must work twice as hard as their white counterparts.
> Lesson #2 - Black folks must always dress professionally. Don't allow white folks to discredit you because of how you are dressed.
> Lesson #3 - You can't fully trust white people. They may appear as though they like and want to help you, but deep inside, they don't value black people.

When I heard my mom and aunts talk like this, it began to shape how I viewed white people and my work ethic. I never once saw them be disrespectful to anyone who was white, but I learned that they knew how to navigate through life in the South.

My grandmother on my mom's side, a God-fearing woman, would always take us to church. And while we were there, she ensured we stayed awake the whole time by giving us a peppermint or an elbow. She made sure we prayed before going to bed and eating any meals or snacks. She was also an educator and always stressed the need for me to enunciate my words and use proper grammar. Every summer, she would grill my sister and me on vocabulary words, ensuring we knew how to speak "proper English." She also taught me a few things.

> Lesson #4 - Speaking properly isn't "talking white."
> It's speaking proper English.
> Lesson #5 - Put the Lord first in all things.

Grandma always made it a point to encourage us as black children in the South. There were days when we would watch the Atlanta Braves play baseball, and on occasion, we would stop watching for a moment, and she would warn me about the dangers I would face in life, but she also taught me to trust in God. She was the one who taught me that life would not always be easy and that I would not win at everything. She did that because I tended to have temper tantrums when I lost a game or didn't get my way. Through my grandmother, I learned the most about Jesus growing up and that no matter what I faced in life, with His help, I could overcome it.

When it comes to family and other lessons learned, I especially enjoyed going to my father's family reunions in Clarksdale, MS, because all the things I loved (family, sports, and soul food) were in the same place at the same time. At the family reunions, most of that side of the family disliked white people. I would hear stories of how black people would be lynched at night. Others would share how they had been mistreated by white police officers, overlooked for jobs or job promotions because they were black, how white people would denigrate them, and how white people would smile in their faces only to stab them in the back when they did not follow orders. To sum it up, attending family reunions taught me some other lessons.

> Lesson #6 - No matter how nice they are, you can't trust white people.
> Lesson #7 - White people only look out for other white people.

Lesson #8 - White people think they are superior to black people.

Because of all this, I believe my parents did their best to keep me in all-black environments so I would not experience racism. But growing up and learning these lessons taught me to keep a close eye on white people and not trust them at an early age. Yet, with the little I knew about God from my grandmother, I figured white people couldn't be that bad. However, when I was about 11 years old, life as I knew it would change. My friend and I were playing and decided to go for a walk. While we were walking, a red pickup truck drove by us, and a white guy in the back yelled, "Get out of the street nigger!"

I had always heard that word used by black folks as a form of greeting, and I knew it was a word white people used to disparage black people, but I had never been called that name. When my mom would use it, she would use it for anyone, regardless of ethnicity. To her, anyone could be a "nigger" because it was more about having an ignorant character, and I would often use the word the same way she did. So when the guy yelled at me, my response back to him without thinking was, "Yo momma a nigger." The driver of the truck stopped, turned around, and started chasing us.

My friend and I started running back to my house, but we figured we couldn't go directly home or they would know where I lived. So, as these guys were chasing us, we got off the main street, ran through some backyards, and hid. Once the coast was clear, we ran home and didn't tell a soul what happened. My eyes were finally opened to racism in the South, and eventually, a deep-rooted mistrust of all things white grew. Every racist moment after that reinforced my thinking, and my hatred toward white people became more visceral.

When I was in high school, my mom laid down some additional rules. Among them were these two commandments:

#1 - Don't date white girls.

#2 - Don't get a white girl pregnant.

These two commandments weren't just about sex. Rather, they were about protecting me. My mom knew if a white father knew I was seeing their daughter in any way, more than likely, nothing good would come from it. By this time, I was well aware of people in the historical South who were murdered, like Emmet Till, after being accused of offending white women. I did not want to end up like that. However, with all of my hormones, the only thing my high school brain processed was that it was okay to have sex with white girls as long as I didn't get them pregnant, didn't bring them around my mom, and the white girl's family didn't know we were together. But even with these rules, I learned that you can't trust white people, and you definitely should not have relationships with them.

Shortly after starting college, I took a young lady home one night in my Toyota Celica. It was a lovely black sports car with chrome rims, tinted windows, and a sound system with just the right amount of bass so people could hear me coming down the street. While I was driving, I heard sirens and got pulled over. The officer, who was white, asked if I knew why I was being pulled over. "No, Sir," I replied, "I was just taking my friend home." He told me I was speeding, but I knew I wasn't. He then asked me to step out of the car, and I guess since I wasn't moving fast enough, he yanked the door open, pulled me out of the vehicle, and slammed me on the hood of the car. The young lady I was with started yelling at the officer, and he told her to "shut up." As I was bent over on the car's hood, he asked me where I was going. I told him I was taking her home and then going home. After frisking me, he told me to get back in the car and let me go with a warning. (Yes, all of that for a warning.) As I drove home, I decided that night that white people were the worst thing God ever created.

About five years later, I became a Christian working in corporate America, and my worldview was still the same. God had reconciled me to Himself, but I did not want to be reconciled to whites because I felt it was too risky. I had experienced too much racism, and the trauma of it all still lingered deep within me. But because of my upbringing, I could hide my true feelings towards white people. Like some other black folks in corporate America, I wore a mask and played the white corporate game. I was always friendly and professional toward them, but I was always apprehensive of them.

In 2003, the Lord called me to attend seminary to pursue a Master of Divinity degree. While in seminary, I worshiped alongside white people and sang "white-styled" worship songs (contemporary Christian music) for the first time. This is how I knew that God had a sense of humor. He sent me to a place where I would have to make peace with my enemy. I remember thinking that the songs were so dull and dry. The traditional black church was all I knew, and it seemed like what they were singing in seminary wasn't really worship because it lacked soul and passion. But I did it anyway because it was a requirement.

During my time in seminary, I got to know some white students who seemed genuine, but in the back of my mind, I still felt that I couldn't trust them. The past was once again haunting me. After graduating from seminary, I interviewed for a job as a recruiter at the same seminary. My interviewer, Pam, was the same person who accepted me in the seminary as a Master of Divinity student. She was pleasant to talk with during the interview, and we had a great time. She hired me, and my goal was never to give her an excuse to fire me.

The longer I worked there, the stronger my relationship got with Pam. I would talk with her and her husband, Steve, and I could feel God tearing down my prejudicial worldview through those conversations. Pam and Steve cared about me as a Christian man, not just a black man. Though they were white, they were aware of the black struggle and were not ashamed to admit to other things they did not understand about the unique challenges faced by black folks. They listened to me and never took a position of superiority over me. They were older than me but never looked down on me. Pam and Steve were intentionally building a kingdom relationship with me, and I started to feel like I could trust them with my struggles.

As a recruiter, I had to speak with students of all ethnicities. I would sit and listen to their stories of brokenness and redemption. To my surprise, some of their brokenness was similar to mine. They had experienced trauma, including racism, tribalism, classism, and sexism. After being a recruiter for a while, coworkers would randomly ask me questions about black people. I did nothing unusual that prompted them to ask me questions. I just liked my job and always remained professional. I guess they trusted me. I remember thinking, "What in the world is going on? Why are white folks interested in black people? Do they think I know all black people?" Their questions upset me because they always seemed to start with, "Why do black people..." and since I was working in a predominately white environment, I never felt safe to say what I wanted to say. I thought that they did not care about the plight of black folks and just wanted black students to help bolster seminary enrollment. I felt like what I learned about white people growing up was being reinforced. But then I met Michael.

While I was recruiting Michael to the seminary, we would meet and talk about general issues around race. I did not immediately tell him my views about white people because I recruited him into the seminary. As time went on, Michael and I started developing a solid friendship. Later on, we started working together at the seminary. He shared his journey as a pastor, husband, and father. His transparency and honesty were surprisingly refreshing. He articulated things I struggled with, and he began pastoring me. I shared my struggles with him, and he never betrayed my trust. Even though I grew up with a disdain for white people, while in seminary, God orchestrated different scenarios where I had white people like Pam, Steve, and Michael who would listen to and advocate for me during some of my darkest moments in life. They walked with me through significant emotional events that eventually helped me become a better man, pastor, husband, and father. Michael would soon become my best friend, brother, and pastor. We talked about everything from church to fatherhood. We went to conferences together, and I allowed him fully into my world. He saw the best and worst of me. Because of these experiences, all of the lessons I learned at an early age were being dismantled. The Holy Spirit was demolishing my selfish worldview. Mental health counseling professor Larry Wagner once wrote:

> For believers, the ability to change comes when we put our faith in Christ, and a unique, powerful change agent is turned loose on our "I": the Holy Spirit. His primary goal is to remove all influences of the old "I" and replace them with his presence.[5]

Author and minister Henry Van Dyke once said, "Self is the only prison that can bind the soul." Our spiritual bondage to self perpetuates the division, hurt, and mistrust while simultaneously fueling the enemy's plans. But how is this possible? How can someone who calls themselves a Christian still live in the bondage of worldly thinking? I believe that it begins with many not understanding that, as believers, we have been made alive with Christ and have a new nature that is opposed to the mistreatment of others made in the image of God. When I decided to follow Jesus, I did not embrace that I was a new creation, that I needed to begin to see the world differently, and that I needed to treat **ALL** people differently. I just wanted eternal life. I was doing my best to hold on to what I had learned growing up. But over time and interacting with people different from me, I realized, "Therefore, if anyone is in Christ, he is a new creation. The old has passed away; behold, the new has come," (2 Cor.5:17).

For those crucified with Christ, we have died to the old life, ungodly thoughts, worldly principles, and biased ideologies that promote disunity. However, we must realize that proclaiming death to the old nature and living like you're dead in the freedom of the new nature are two different things. If we give lip service and proclaim that we have died and have a new nature but never live it out, we will continue to have veiled conversations and never achieve unity with others. As Christians, we resurrect the old nature and build walls between us and others when we allow ourselves to be controlled by the past and secular ideas that run counter to the gospel. The results of resurrecting the old nature are also seen when we see Christians demonize other Christians for having preferences, opinions, political positions, theology, and values that differ from their own.

The problem is that we have sacrificed charity for one another for the sake of being right. And yes, at times, we may be right, but truth communicated at the wrong time and without love is brutality. Some churches are becoming places that are breeding and harboring brutal old-natured believers. But this is not what God has called us to do. Because of faith in Jesus, God has now called us to walk in the new life He has given us. Ephesians 4:17-24 should challenge us to embrace the new life in Christ:

> [17] Now this I say and testify in the Lord, that you must no longer walk as the Gentiles do, in the futility of their minds. [18] They are darkened in their understanding, alienated from the life of God because of the ignorance that is in them, due to their hardness of heart. [19] They have become callous and have given themselves up to sensuality, greedy to practice every kind of impurity. [20] But that is not the way you learned Christ!— [21] assuming that you have heard about him and were taught in him, as the truth is in Jesus, [22] to put off your old self, which belongs to your former manner of life and is corrupt through deceitful desires, [23] and to be renewed in the spirit of your minds, [24] and to put on the new self, created after the likeness of God in true righteousness and holiness

Let's face it, many of us grew up learning some lessons that have caused us to act in ungodly ways. We all are products of what we learned in our families and other environments, whether good or bad. And we carry all of that bias and baggage into our relationship with Jesus. Sometimes, we'll have a moment of surrendering, but the old flesh and habits tend to creep back and reveal themselves again.

There is something freeing about realizing and admitting how your past has shaped who you are as a person and acknowledging the dysfunction that exists. It is also therapeutic when you know how you interact with people is often based on those past experiences. But breaking from the bondage of the past is one of the most challenging things to do as followers of Jesus.

I challenge you to consider whether your worldview may be distorted in some way. I also encourage you to think about what experiences happened in the past and what lessons you were taught that shaped your way of thinking. When I considered my experiences with white people and women, I realized that the past ungodly experiences were simply tricks of the enemy to keep me from being in a healthy community with others. It is a very subtle trick designed to have believers walk in anger, fear, and not faith. We have to stop putting faith in the experience and start putting it in the Lord, who has redeemed us. If we are going to die to ourselves and seek unity with others, we cannot nourish old ways, old thinking, and old habits. We must be willing to embrace communities and people who do not look, think, or act like us. And if we have experienced trauma, we must get help to deal with it.

Don't get me wrong; I understand that we go through a sanctification process as believers, and going through that process means there will sometimes be disappointment when the old nature rears its ugly head. Some of us still have the mental sin residue and emotional pain that needs to be healed. Yet, God still calls us to live holy as He is holy. God's work in our hearts doesn't stop at salvation. It is an ongoing process of renewing our minds, shedding the old nature, and embracing the new.

In Ephesians 4:17, we read that walking in the old life is futile. In other words, if a believer continues to live according to their old life, they are devoid of truth no matter who they are and are still in mental darkness. Romans 6:8 tells us, "that we have died with Christ." By embracing my death at salvation, I am now free to love others, be patient with them, grow in the knowledge of God, and be conformed to the image of Christ. Romans 8:29 tells us, "For those whom he foreknew he also predestined to be conformed to the image of his Son, in order that he might be the firstborn among many brothers."[6] We are called to imitate Jesus in every way, especially as we relate to those who are different from us or have hurt us. In order to connect to and love them, we must let go of our old nature, the pain, and the lessons we learned that do not reflect Jesus. And we must put on our new life in Christ and walk alongside others, in love, with a new heart.

Up to this point, I've outlined how my journey from harboring prejudice and mistrust towards white people to forming deep and godly relationships with them was a process. It required God's intervention, some divine appointments with people unlike myself, and my willingness to be honest about struggles. I pray that this chapter has helped some to realize and served as a reminder for others that no matter where we've come from, what we have learned, or what our experiences have been, God's transformative work has no limits.

In the chapters ahead, I encourage you to keep an open heart and a teachable spirit, knowing that God can take the broken pieces of your past and create a masterpiece of unity, love, and understanding.

3

People Suck

> *And I said: "Woe is me! For I am lost; for I am a man of unclean lips, and I dwell in the midst of a people of unclean lips; for my eyes have seen the King, the LORD of hosts!*
> — Isaiah 6:5

The words spoken in Isaiah 6:5 came after Isaiah saw God in the splendor of His holiness. He no longer saw God as something familiar and ordinary. Instead, he saw God as extraordinary and sublime. As Isaiah heard the angels echoing the hallowedness of God, his first response was one of deep self-reflection. Isaiah realized that God was truly holy and he was not worthy of being in His presence. From this revelation of God, his only recourse was confession. No longer is Isaiah blind to his wretched spiritual condition or the depraved spiritual condition of the people. He now understands how gravely he and the people have fallen short of God's holiness. In other words, Isaiah realized that *people suck and God is good*.

Isaiah's revelation and consequent confession put his heart in tune with God's frequency of love and grace. Shortly after, an angel cleanses Isaiah by placing a hot coal on his lips (Isaiah 6:6-7). By doing so, Isaiah's sin is atoned for, and his guilt is taken away. Isaiah is no longer an enemy of God, and his heart is primed to accept the role of God's prophet to the people. Confession was pivotal in Isaiah's transformation; however, it only came after the revelation of God's holiness. Seeing, knowing, and believing God is part of the process, but confessing sin is the catalyst to living out God's call and commission to reach and love others. The revelation from this passage was critical to my journey of overcoming self to live in unity with others, but I still struggled.

Larry Wagner once wrote, "Even when we recognize the moment of decision and desire to respond positively to the Spirit, the ensuing struggle reveals how hard the old nature fights to remain in control."[7] As the Lord was dismantling the prejudices I had learned growing up, I still held on to the old nature of distrusting my white brothers and sisters. I was in an ongoing internal battle to walk in love and peace with people unlike myself. I still viewed the world through my biases while in seminary and attending church. Reflecting on my condition prompted me to confess:

> "Lord, forgive me for hating white people. Forgive me for not trusting white people who are your children. Forgive me for my prejudice towards white people. Forgive me for the way I have viewed women. Lord, lead me to love all people. Lead me to better relationships with everyone regardless of skin color and gender. Help me to see them the way you see them."

After I confessed to the Lord in 2009, I was introduced to multicultural ministry and began to appreciate the uniqueness of different cultures and varying points of view. I started reading about cultural intelligence and the value of diversity. I was introduced to books on culture and reconciliation by authors such as John Perkins, David Livermore, John Piper, Tim Keller, Tony Evans, Efrem Smith, and Brenda Salter-McNeil. I started learning more about being a peacemaker with people who have different cultures, interests, and worldviews. As I was learning that same year, I was called on to teach a class to international students to help them perfect their English, expose them to other cultures, and teach them what it means to love people cross-culturally.

Little did I know that the entire class would be composed of Christian Korean students. During the course, we discussed stereotypes, cultural differences, personal struggles, generational gaps, and socioeconomic differences among Koreans in Korea. As the students shared their experiences, it opened my eyes to the division and damage happening worldwide within the church. This prompted me to read more articles and go to conferences about reconciliation. My theology and worldview were starting to align more with God's word and heart. I became more discerning that when people from all walks of life and perspectives come to God on His terms, He unconditionally embraces them.

From then on, I started seeking out diverse relationships and embraced people from all cultures and backgrounds. Later on, I had opportunities to speak at various multiethnic events. I began preaching at transitional homes for ex-offenders and embraced people with backgrounds ranging from homelessness to upper class. I was excited to see how God was using me to minister across cultural, social, and socioeconomic boundaries. He was taking me on a journey to create spaces of unity and peace with people from all walks of life. I had come to see that we are all unclean in one way or another, but we can all truly live as one in the body of Christ. In my mind, I was becoming a champion for unity, especially in the church, because I knew that God could do it and wanted His church to reflect His kingdom. But then, something catastrophic happened.

After countless engagements of preaching, teaching, and relationship building, I was getting emotionally and spiritually drained because it felt like nothing was changing. When Trayvon Martin died in 2012, I saw the church divisions slowly returning. Some thought Trayvon Martin's death was murder, while others thought it was self-defense. Then came Eric Garner, Michael Brown, Eurie Martin, and Botham Jean. After that, it seemed that the pastors and church leaders I met with had no desire to embrace diversity because of the building racial tension in the country. I also grew weary of hearing polarizing viewpoints that underscored deep divisions across racial, socioeconomic, educational, theological, and ideological lines. It seemed to me that the church was becoming more and more divided.

I thought to myself, "Can't they see it? Don't they understand that we, God's people, must be and live as one?" I was getting upset, not realizing that I was the same way at one point. It's funny how we quickly call out the way others are but forget that is how we used to be. This continued to fuel my frustration about the division in the church, but like any "good" Christian, I hid it. I never talked to anyone about it because I felt they wouldn't understand.

As time passed, in 2019, overflowing with frustration, I decided to visit author and civil rights activist Dr. John Perkins in Jackson, MS. I had read almost all of his books, and there I was, sitting in his living room at his Bible study. He spoke about how the gospel was about loving people and how only love can bring people together. He shared that we all must fight for reconciliation, regardless of our ethnic background. He shared that we must focus on community and not just individualism. I remember asking, "Because there is still division in the church, why do you continue to fight?" I needed to know the answer to this question. Why should I keep fighting a battle that appears can never be won? His response was, "Jesus Christ compels me to love. I have to love. Love is the only way."

As I drove back to Columbia, SC, I pondered the response of Dr. Perkins, but my anger would not let me receive his answer. Still feeling overwhelmed and discouraged, I had concluded that I was done. No one wants peace. No one gives grace. Living in unity involves too much sacrifice and love. It calls for people to get involved in the messy lives of others and grow together on a day-to-day basis. Unification and peace are more than just people coming together; it calls for appreciating and embracing the differences we all have while at the same time walking our faith journeys together while elevating and embracing those differences for the glory of God. But I did not want to do that.

"Forget what Dr. Perkins said," I thought, "White people will never understand the struggle. Non-whites will always have to tolerate mistreatment. Most black people will never get involved to help solve the issue out of fear. Latinos and Asians will always feel invisible in the conversation. The church will always be divided. There will always be black churches, white churches, Asian churches and Latino churches, liberal churches, conservative churches, rich churches, and poor churches. Issues will continue to divide the people of God." For the past 30-plus years of being stereotyped, suffering harassment by the police, seeing churches ethnically divided, and hearing sermons that socially divided people, I just decided to tolerate the division that existed. It had become my belief that peace and unity weren't possible in the church or the world.

Dr. Martin Luther King Jr. once said, "To answer the question, 'Where do we go from here?' ...we must first honestly recognize where we are now."[8] With all of my irritation at the division in the church, I woke up one and went to my backyard at 6:30 a.m. As I started my quiet time, I directed all of my anger, pain, disgust, and growing apathy toward the church toward the Lord, and I asked Him, "When will the division end? When will the church get it right and stop with the racism, classism, sexism, lack of grace, and beating each other up?" I am not sure what happens in your devotional time with the Lord, but too often in my quiet time, when I ask the Lord about someone else or inquire why some people do what they do, He inevitably puts the focus back on me. On this particular occasion, I was convicted by the Holy Spirit because He revealed that:

1. My question was accusing the Lord of allowing all of this sin to continue as if that was God's desire.
2. I was treating this issue of division as if it was too difficult for God.
3. I was exalting myself above those who struggle with accepting others. I thought I was better than them.

That morning, as the Lord searched the depths of my heart, He shared my actual condition with me. It was kind of like when my mom bought my first car. It was a 1988 blue Ford Escort. When she bought it, I tinted the windows, put a sound system in it, and put shiny hubcaps on it. I called my car "blue funk." The problem with blue funk was that my mom bought it in "as-is" condition. I didn't know that the "as-is" condition also meant there were other issues with the car.

It wasn't until I spent time driving blue funk that I realized that the heat and air conditioning didn't work. It constantly needed spark plugs, and it consistently leaked oil. On the outside, I dressed it up, but under the hood, after spending time driving it for a while, I realized that blue funk was a mess. As I spent time with God that morning, He started giving me a better perspective of how broken I was, and I saw my as-is condition.

Amid my conviction, the Lord reminded me that I was no better than the people I prayed for. They have their brokenness, just like I do. Then it hit me. One of the reasons why unity is so hard is because we all hide our sins and put on a mask of perfection until something happens to pull the ugly out of us. We all have issues and biases that we struggle with but remain silent about. Some of those biases can be seen, and some can't. Some of us even place our bias in its special "bias compartment." We have become so desensitized to it that we forget that it is bias and sin. Others treat it as if it is not biased to begin with.

We justify it by saying things like, "That is just who I am," or "That is how I grew up.". And because we are so imperfect, our sinful nature will not allow us to see how bad we are. So, the only way to even scratch the surface of eradicating division in the church is for us as people to come face-to-face with God, see and lament our condition, and confess. This is the catalyst for changing the human heart. French writer and theologian Francois Fenelon once said, "We can often do more for other men by trying to correct our own faults than by trying to correct theirs."

As Christians, we cannot hide or protect our sins. We must die to self, go through a daily renewal, see God for who He truly is, and see our sins for what they truly are. We must also allow God to examine our hearts and intentions. Psalm 139:23 says, "Search me, O God, and know my heart! Try me and know my thoughts!" If we genuinely seek the Lord, He will show us the error of our ways, the condition of our hearts, the blindspots we ignore, and His righteousness that we are to live out.

The Response

On that humbling morning, the Lord responded to my prayer as He did for Isaiah. He reminded me of how awesome, boundless, infinite, and unlimited He is. I was reminded of the following scriptures:

Job 12:13
"With God are wisdom and might; he has counsel and understanding..."

1 Samuel 2:6-8
⁶ The Lord kills and brings to life; he brings down to Sheol and raises up. ⁷ The Lord makes poor and makes rich; he brings low and he exalts. ⁸ He raises up the poor from the dust; he lifts the needy from the ash heap to make them sit with princes and inherit a seat of honor. For the pillars of the earth are the Lord's, and on them he has set the world.

Romans 11:33-36
³³ Oh, the depth of the riches and wisdom and knowledge of God! How unsearchable are his judgments and how inscrutable his ways! ³⁴ "For who has known the mind of the Lord, or who has been his counselor?"

> ³⁵ "Or who has given a gift to him that he might be repaid?" ³⁶ For from him and through him and to him are all things. To him be glory forever. Amen.

God's name flows to the end of the earth. He knows exactly what He is doing and does not, nor will he ever, need my advice. He is entirely self-sufficient and self-existing. As the creator, sustainer, redeemer, provider, and resurrector, the Lord has all authority in heaven and on earth. He is the one who has prepared every day of our lives before we are even born. Power and might are in his hand, and I have no right to question the potter as the clay. And when I do, my questions should still be asked out of humility and reverence for Him. Theologian A.W. Tozer once wrote:

> "When I was explaining the infinitude of God, I pointed out that there are no degrees in God. God is not at the top of the heap in an ever-ascending perfection of being, from the worm on up until finally we reach God. On the contrary, God is completely different and separate, so that there are no degrees in God. God is simply God, an infinite perfection of fullness, and we cannot say God is a little more or a little less. "More" and "less" are creature words. We can say that a man has a little more strength today than yesterday. We can say the child is a little taller this year; he's growing. But you can't apply more or less to God, For God is the perfect One; He's just God."[9]

These words should serve as a reminder of how awesome God is and how we are to revere Him.

The Reflection

By reflecting on all that God had done, His character, and meditating on His Word, a door for self-discovery was opened for me. Sitting on my patio in the backyard, I started to see my sinful views of people and my lack of humility in that prayer time. I saw how my lack of self-awareness crippled me spiritually and emotionally, and all I did was use the crutch of pride to hold myself up. It's mind-blowing how often God's holiness exposes our blind spots. John Calvin, a theologian, and pastor, touched on this point in The Institutes of Christian Religion:

> "...it is evident that man never attains to a true self-knowledge until he has previously contemplated the face of God and come down after such contemplation to look into himself. For (such is our innate pride) we always seem to ourselves just, and upright, and wise, and holy, until we are convinced, by clear evidence, of our injustice, vileness, folly, and impurity. Convinced, however, we are not, if we look to ourselves only, and not to the Lord also — He being the only standard by the application of which this conviction can be produced."[10]

When we go before a holy God, our humanity comes into contact with God's divinity. We will see our flaws because God is in the business of using His holiness to expose our darkness so we can walk in the light of Christ's righteousness.

As you read this, you may be tempted to think, "I am not the problem," or "Other people need to get their act together." If you have made these comments, you have exalted yourself in some fashion, but you are not the only one. We naturally promote ourselves and think we are righteous in our own eyes. We must all realize that by exalting things, even oneself, in addition to or instead of God, we have contributed directly or indirectly to the divide that has infiltrated the church. Some of us promote our past hurts, giving them power over us. In the words of theologian Kosuke Koyama, "Let's be critical about ourselves. The

Christian faith demands such self-criticism."[11] We must realize that we tend to manage our sins and exalt things that are not Christ-like, which further fuels the disunity within the church. We also allow events and trauma to define us. Some of us have even exalted the shame we walk in.

The same happened with Isaiah and the nation of Israel. Isaiah's revelation from God came when King Uzziah died. Author and pastor Raymond Ortlund Jr. once wrote:

> God lavished success on His people. But they did not handle it well. They continued to affirm the traditional faith, but God himself became unreal to them. Uzziah sought God for a while; but when he was strong, "he grew proud to his destruction" (2 Chronicles 26:5, 16). The whole nation followed their king into complacency, and God's patience with them finally ran out. Uzziah's death marked the end of an era... It was at just such a defining moment that Isaiah was called into the ministry...[12]

When King Uzziah died, the false exalted glory of Israel died. Israel's hope was in King Uzziah. Yes, they, too, exalted God and something else. And for Isaiah to truly see God, the king of Israel had to die. This begs for a time of self-criticism. What has to die in your life for you to see God for who He is and His agenda for what it truly is? Have you been hypocritical in your dealings with others? What is within your fallen nature that you must allow God to annihilate? What do you exalt along with God? What is your bias?

The death of these ungodly ideologies, stereotypes, and idols is the only way to see God for who He truly is, which allows Him to renew and influence us through the power of the Holy Spirit. If a person chooses to follow Christ, He must first deny himself (Luke 9:23). That is the only response to the revelation of the greatness of God. If we are going to fight for unity in the church, the first fight is with our hearts. We must own up to our contributions to this dilemma. Being released from our spiritual bondage and blindspots starts with us. We must believe and demonstrate that all of us are equal in the sight of God. As God's children, all of us are on a journey of transformation, and our issues boil down to one thing – selfishness.

Seeing God in the beauty of His holiness and greatness should let us see how weak and vile we all are. Too often, in our pride, we quickly judge those who wrestle with a sin that we don't usually wrestle with. This leads us to be intolerant of people. I say that because that was me. As I asked the Lord, when will your children stop being separated, and when will division end in Your church? He responded, "When will you stop doing what you are doing?"

It was not the answer I wanted to hear but it was the correct response. Jesus said in John 13:34-35, "A new commandment I give to you that you love one another: just as I have loved you, you also are to love one another. By this, all people will know that you are my disciples if you have love for one another." In my prayer time, I realized I had violated this new commandment. I had not been charitable with my brothers and sisters like Jesus has been and continues to be with me. Jesus has been patient, gracious, and merciful with me. And yet, I had not given others that same patience, grace, and mercy.

As I sat on the patio in the early morning, I lamented over my weakness and the divisions in the church. And as I began to repent of my self-righteousness, the Lord directed me to Lamentations 3:21-24:

> "But this I call to mind, and therefore I have hope:
> The steadfast love of the Lord never ceases;
> his mercies never come to an end; they are new every
> morning; great is your faithfulness.
> "The Lord is my portion," says my soul,
> "therefore I will hope in him."

After praying and crying out to the Lord, I opened my eyes and had more hope. I thought about others who had come before me, already fighting to unite the church. I thought about people who have devoted much of their lives to seeing unity within the body of Christ. God reminded me that I was not the only one fighting this fight and that He had never disengaged from the battle. I also realized that this would not be a quick fix because people cannot be fixed; people can only be transformed, and that transformation, as it has been for me, is a slow process.

After reading Lamentations 3:21-24, I had to give up thinking my ways were the right ways and remember that God is the one who is in control of all things. He knows what He is doing. I also realized that the current reality and condition of the church do not hinder the sovereignty of God, His faithfulness, and His redemptive plan. In the same vein, when it comes to this journey of unification, I, along with everyone who wants to fight, can get back up and fight no matter how many times we have been knocked down. Love calls us to fight, and God calls us as His ambassadors to throw off the things that hinder us and run the race He has marked out for us.

The principle of self-discovery only happens in stages. It is a seed and watering process that unfolds in God's time. During this process, there are times when God will cultivate and nurture the fruit being produced in us and use it to bless others. Then, there are other times when He will prune and weed out the blind spots that hinder us and the apprehensions that keep us from engaging with others who are different. This process only happens when we take the time and go before the Lord with all our mess. In these moments with the Lord, we lay every aspect of our lives on His altar. Lamentations 3:40 says, "Let us test and examine our ways and return to the Lord!"

Some people continuously show selfishness, arrogance, entitlement, victimization, and defeatism. If the Holy Spirit dwells in you, you know in your heart that your way of living and stronghold is a burden. And what has this way of living helped to accomplish for the kingdom of God? Self-awareness is recognizing where we are and admitting that we need help to bring glory to the Lord. Jesus is there to offer Himself because He wants to engage in a great exchange with you.

He wants to give you His love, rest, compassion, patience, and peace in exchange for your burdens. This is the heart of Jesus. He already knows that you are struggling. He wants you to lean into Him with all of your broken desires and ideologies so that He can begin to renew you, break down the walls in your life, and give you life. We come to Him broken so that we can be made whole. The more we are engaged in the world's ways, the more we will become bankrupt in our thinking.

But the more we focus on the Kingdom of God and spend time in His presence, the more we will be enlightened to God's divine agenda of ethnic unity. What do you need to step back from to engage in a great exchange with Jesus? Perhaps you must step away from specific media, work, or even church. To truly experience God and give Him those things that cripple us, we need to step away from the world to see how messed up we are.

I saw how bad I was and how judgmental I had become on that early morning. If we are ever going to become mature Christians who grow from the counsel of God's Word, then we need to devote intentional time to present ourselves as a sacrifice to the Lord so that He can renew our thinking. This process of stepping back for mind renewal is a life-long process.

If we are going to be thoroughly altered in a way that brings unity and peace to the church, then we must go to our desolate places and commune with the Father. As we commune with Him, He will show us how we have lazily abdicated our responsibility to pursue oneness in the body of Christ. Sitting before the Father is the beginning of seeking unity. As we abide with the Lord and become immersed in the scriptures, we will begin to see God's heart for oneness among His people. As we delight in Him, His desires will eventually become our desires over time. However, if we allow ourselves to be arrested by social media, politics, generational ideologies, or social causes, we will not have any margin for focusing on the Lord. Stepping back to chase after the righteousness of God is paramount if we as a church are going to walk as one.

In the fight for unity in the church, as followers of Jesus, we are both the problem and the solution. Will you lament with me, confess, repent, and go on a lifelong journey of self-discovery to pursue peace and unity in the church? If the answer is yes, let's continue the fight and go one more round to fight for ethnic unity in the church. If the answer is no, go before the Lord so He can show you what's really in your heart. It is my prayer that after you spend time with the Lord, you will see your "as-is" condition, begin the renewal process, understand the part you play in the problem, know that you are the solution, and realize how powerful we are as a church when we live as one for His glory.

4

The Monster in the Mirror

> *For they all seek their own interests, not those of Jesus Christ.* — **Philippians 2:21**

In 2020, Nate Gunter wrote a book titled "Me Monster." In the book, a child demonstrates selfish behavior with other children while playing with them and even at home with his parents. He acted out so much that no one wanted to be around him. When he asked his parents why no one wanted to play with him, his dad beat his chest and said, "ME, ME, ME, ME." His dad said, "Why would anyone want to be with a Me Monster? The Me Monster is the one who is selfish and mean, and you are a Me Monster!..."[13] The dirty truth is that the church is filled with Me Monsters.

As a teenager, I tried boxing twice. The first time was when I was 15. I met a guy in the gym, saw him boxing, and asked if we could spar a little. After he sized me up, he agreed. From his nonchalant body language, I could tell that he did not perceive me as a threat, so we decided to have at it. As we stood toe to toe, he said, "I'm going to pull my punches so I won't hurt you." I said okay, but in my mind, I thought this would be easy since I had seen boxers like Muhammad Ali and Sugar Ray Leonard move graciously and dodge punches with what seemed like minimal effort. I was so young and naive. Once we started, I noticed my opponent hesitated to punch, so I threw the first punch.

And it was a quick jab. To my surprise, he easily dodged my punch and threw a counterpunch that connected to the side of my face. And even though it was a pulled punch, it hurt so bad that it was his last punch. I recognized that I was no match for this guy, so I quickly did what any sane 15-year-old would do: Quit! Laughing, he said, "No problem, I understand."

Two years later, I was playing with some guys that I knew, and then one of them said, "We should box." And once again, in the back of my mind, I thought this would be easy, plus I had previously been in a ring with a real fighter. So we put the gloves on and started sizing each other up. We moved around in a circle for a bit, and then he threw a punch. I dodged it. I had the reach advantage since I was taller, but he kept his distance. I saw my opportunity, so I moved closer and threw a hook. He side-stepped my punch and hit me with what seemed like a roundhouse. At that moment, I recognized that I was not a fighter. So once again, I did what any sane 17-year-old would do: Quit! All the guys laughed at me, but I didn't care. At least I walked away with only a slight bruise on my face. Reflecting on my brief boxing career, I realized I did not go over one of the first basic fighting rules: know your opponent. I was so focused on myself and what I thought I could do that I never studied my opponent and just jumped into the fight, leading to my amateur boxing record of 0-2.

When we think about the Me Monster we are up against, it is paramount that we know who we are dealing with. They are individuals that only think about themselves. They are all of us. And as a result, when you encounter them with truth, you will quickly find that they are either in the swamp of self-trust or self-preservation.

The Swamp of Self-Trust

Author Lorenzo Scupoli once wrote:

> Distrust of self is so absolutely requisite in the spiritual combat, that without this virtue we cannot expect to defeat our weakest passions, much less gain a complete victory. This important truth should be deeply embedded in our hearts; for, although in ourselves we are nothing, we are too apt to overestimate our own abilities and to conclude falsely that we are of some importance. This vice springs from the corruption of our nature. But the more natural a thing is, the more difficult it is to be discovered.[14]

Before coming to know Jesus as Lord and Savior, Christians were conditioned to be Me Monsters. (Ephesians 2:1-2). And now, as disciples of Christ, we are constantly engaged in spiritual warfare against our meism that was developed in the past, tempting us to think of ourselves more highly than we should. This is one of the greatest battles for the believer. Self-trust goes against the very nature of faith. Proverbs 3:5-6 says, "Trust in the Lord with all your heart and do not lean on your own understanding. In all your ways acknowledge him, and he will make straight your paths."

These verses suggest that, by nature, we tend to lean on our understanding. Because of this natural disposition, we are challenged to acknowledge, recognize, and think carefully about God and what He would have us do. Doing so will make us more conscious of His will and submit to His ways. God knows that when we assume the posture of self-trust, we will begin to believe and proclaim that we have all wisdom and think we can do all things without Him. Once we take on this god complex, we begin to act and think independently of God and drown in the spiritual swamp of self-trust. As we rest on our culture, socio-economic class, political affiliations, and self-righteousness, we dupe ourselves into thinking that we are better than we are. This leaves us vulnerable to creating more division because we eventually forget how prone we are to sin against God and others. Leading us to become more intolerant and impatient with others. As we wear the veil of self-trust, we become paralyzed by our idealism, ideologies, and individual rights. Spiritually, we become impaired from living the way God wants us to and doing what God wants us to do. This is a trap of the enemy because self-trust keeps us dependent on ourselves, even at the expense of others.

As we trust in ourselves, we quickly believe that we are ideologically elite, and we leave no room at the table to collaborate with others who are different. And when those different from us are not allowed to be at the table, we miss out on the richness of experiences that others have and the power that comes from being one. Galatians 2:20 says, "I have been crucified with Christ. It is no longer I who live, but Christ who lives in me. And the life I now live in the flesh I live by faith in the Son of God, who loved me and gave himself for me." If we, as followers of Christ, honestly believe this verse, we must die to self-trust. We must die to our agendas and put God's agenda above everything else. We must also allow Christ to remain supreme over every area of life. Suppose we refuse to do this and continue to put confidence in ourselves. It would demonstrate that valuing God, His ultimate purpose, and people made in His image are no longer a priority. This is the same dilemma that led to the fall of Adam and Eve. The serpent tricked Eve into placing more value on what she thought was pleasing to her instead of what God had said, and Adam placed more value on following Eve than following God's direct words to him. They trusted in themselves, which led to the introduction of sin to all of humanity.

The Swamp of Self-Preservation

One of the mysteries of our human depravity is that we never know just how sinful we are. Even when we give our lives to Jesus, many still cannot fathom the brokenness within them. Yes, we have been declared righteous according to Romans 5:1. But even with our righteous position in Christ, we still fall victim to sin. Dr. Martin Luther King Jr.

once wrote of the Christian: "We can still become so involved in the things of this world that we are unconsciously carried away by the rushing tide of materialism which leaves us treading in the confused waters of secularism."[15]

Frequently, we create clever justifications for our actions; one way we do that is by comparing our sins to the sins of others. The more serious Christian can be so performance-driven that they quickly convince themselves that they are bad, but not that bad based on their service to the Lord. However, we are soberly reminded in Isaiah 64:6 that "we have all become like one who is unclean, and all our righteous deeds are like a polluted garment. We all fade like a leaf, and our iniquities, like the wind, take us away." English author and preacher John Bunyan once wrote:

> Sin is still in us, and with us, and mixes itself with whatever we do, whether what we do be religious or civil: for not only our prayers and our sermons, our hearing and preaching; but our houses, our shops, our trades, and our beds, are all polluted with sin.[16]

In our attempts to create unity in the church, sin is still ever-present within us. In our desire to create environments of unity, we can still use divisive rhetoric that exalts oneself over another. And when things are said, the tendency is not to show grace and mercy. Instead, we revert quickly to self-defense. When people say something we don't like, we can quickly attack instead of first praying about what has happened. When we quickly jump into self-preservation mode, we will immediately focus on intent and not the impact of our actions.

When God called out for Adam after he ate the fruit, Adam went into self-preservation mode: "The woman whom you gave to be with me, she gave me fruit of the tree, and I ate" (Genesis 3:12). Another translation is my own, and goes like this, "Lord it was not my intent to eat the fruit. She just gave it to me." Adam is more concerned about the intent and never asks God about the impact of his actions. Death was the consequence of his actions, yet in Genesis 3, Adam never mentions it. He is only focused on himself. Eve, focusing on herself, did the same thing as she blamed the serpent. When we jump into self-preservation mode, we are only concerned about ourselves and quickly blame others. The impact of our actions is not considered, nor do we extend grace to the person who may have offended us. Dane Ortlund wrote:

> Fallen humans are natural self-advocates. It flows out of us. Self-exonerating, self-defending. We do not need to teach young children to make excuses when they are caught misbehaving. There is a natural built-in mechanism that immediately kicks into gear to explain why it wasn't really their fault. Our fallen hearts intuitively manufacture reasons that our case is not really that bad. The fall is manifested not only in our sinning but in our response to our sinning. We minimize, we excuse, and we explain away. In short, we speak, even if only in our hearts, in our defense. We advocate for ourselves.[17]

One of the hardest pills to swallow is that when I wake up each morning and look in the mirror, I look at someone who has great potential but is also my greatest enemy. I see a person who can be both the hero and the villain. And because I am born in sin, I take on the selfish role of the villain too often. We are all potential villains in our own stories. If we are not careful, we will inevitably create a legacy of division among others by succumbing to our selfishness. Now, you may say, "I am not the villain." However, doctor and minister Martyn Lloyd-Jones would disagree. He wrote:

> You will never make yourself feel that you are a sinner, because there is a mechanism in you as a result of sin that will always be defending you against every accusation. We are all on very good terms with ourselves, and we can always put up a good case for ourselves. Even if we try to make ourselves feel that we are sinners, we will never

do it. There is only one way to know that we are sinners, and that is to have some dim, glimmering conception of God.[18]

In our sinfulness and the swamps of self-trust and self-preservation, we can be both the oppressed and the oppressor. All of us can seek justice and also be the ones that contribute to injustice. We can take mental shortcuts and define people with little information about them instead of taking the mental energy needed to get to know them. And we often let our social norms and the lens through which we see the world prohibit us from truly embracing different people. Authors Spencer Perkins and Chris Rice informed us of this by writing:

> Our social blinders result in subtle and careless patterns, traditions, and systems that encourage racial separation and inequality remain unnoticed, intact, and unchallenged. They even seem normal. We need to take a look at the institutions that shape our thinking.[19]

When we are singularly focused on ourselves, our worldview becomes solely based on how we see things. Dr. Michael Heath, one of my best friends who has helped me in my journey, once said, "One of the reasons we continuously struggle with unification is that we always keep the focus on us. We always think of I and me." That is the essence of selfishness. Selfishness says, "I want what I want when I want it, and it does not matter how it affects you." That is the Me Monster. When we get caught up in a culture of "Me," we are only motivated by what makes us feel good or what we think is important. It can happen to the best of us. But how can you determine who is a Me Monster or who isn't? That, my friends, is no small task.

In the 1995 crime thriller *The Usual Suspects,* five criminals are arrested, but none are found guilty. The criminals then decide to take revenge against the police. As the movie goes on, things take a turn because all the criminals have betrayed Keyser Söze, a criminal mastermind who has never been seen. His identity is unknown to the criminal world. After the revenge crime is completed and a trail of bodies is left, the question they and the police have is, "Who is Keyser Söze?" SPOILER ALERT: In the end, one of the five criminals is Keyser Söze. The enemy was in their midst, talking and communing with them the whole time. We must realize that the enemy is not distant as we pursue unity. He, she or they may be closer than many think.

Are you or is someone you know Keyser Söze? Who is the Me Monster? Here are some indicators from my experience to help you answer that question.

Indicator #1 - Everything is okay.

As you talk to people about the issues of division within the church, some seem to think everything is okay and seem oblivious to the division that exists in the church and the impact it has created. These individuals think it is okay to have segregated or diverse churches as long as everyone is saved, worships the Lord, and assimilates into the dominant culture of the church. If approached about the subject of division in the church and the things that cause division, they will say something like, "That is the world's problem; we just have to focus on the gospel." Often, these individuals have never spent time lamenting about the lack of oneness in the church. Pastor Mark Vroegop said:

"Simply stated, lamenting is prayer in pain that leads to trust. Laments are more than mere expressions of sorrow. The goal of lament is to recommit oneself to hoping in God, believing His promises, and a godly response to pain, suffering, and injustice. Lament is the historic biblical prayer language of Christians in pain. It's the voice of God's people while living in a broken world. Laments acknowledge the reality of pain while trusting in God's promises."[20]

Based on Vroegop's definition of lamenting, these Me Monsters will never turn to God regarding disunity in the church because they don't see the reality of division or the pain it causes, and they think everything is okay the way it is.

Indicator #2 - Hearer but not a doer

As a father, I have told my children to take the trash out many times. And yet there are many times, even after telling them, that I will go into the kitchen later in the day and see the trash can still full. They heard me but did not do what I told them to do. In my frustration, I tend to forget that even my children are Me Monsters.

Some Christians can be like this. For some, it is easy to hear the truth but hard to apply it. Anyone who refuses to apply the truth after hearing it only deceives themselves. To blend in with others, they may wear a mask of unity and act like they want to apply what they have learned. However, they will never put into practice what they have been taught. Perhaps it is because the personal cost and sacrifice to apply the truth is too high. Regardless of the reason, they are careful listeners, but after hearing the truth, they will walk away and never apply what they have just learned.

Indicator # 3 - Not Teachable

This, by far, may be the most significant indicator of them all. If someone is overly attached to their way of thinking, they will be short-sighted or have little to no desire to pursue oneness in the church. These Me Monsters refuse to listen. Their viewpoints can sometimes be categorized as myopic, maybe delusional, and they have learned to shut down the truth because they don't see the need to change. In summary, these are fools, and based on Proverbs 1:7, fools despise wisdom and instruction. This indicator is nothing new. God spoke about the nation of Israel when he said, "These people draw near to Me with their mouths and honor Me with their lips, but their hearts are far from Me..." (Isaiah 29:13). With this lack of humility, these Me Monsters will never bring themselves or their worldview before the Lord. Still, they will have no problem telling everyone else they are wrong. Even when approached by truth, they will constantly defend their position regardless of whom it hurts and, through their hardened heart, will likely justify anything threatening the way they see the world.

Usual Suspects

So we come back to the following question. Who Is Keyser Söze? Who is the Me Monster? If you didn't realize it by now, the truth is that it can be any of us. All of us can be the culprit. We all have a small lurking Me Monster deep inside of us that thinks we are better than others. All of us allow the past to dictate our present condition. The problem of division in the church starts with our internal struggles as followers of Jesus. If we embrace our new and true identities in Christ, we are more likely to see our contributions to bigotry, bias, and prejudice in the church. We will recognize our weaknesses and be more willing to lay them on God's altar daily as the Holy Spirit is renewing us. Our willingness to go through ongoing seasons of self-annihilation is critical to the mission of oneness. If we are aware that we are the usual suspects and are all prone to live out our prejudice or old way of thinking, we may become more of the solution than the problem. Francois Fenelon puts it brilliantly when he wrote:

> As you read a passage from the Scriptures, pause after each verse or phrase to hear what God might be saying. Consider how Jesus practices what you are reading. Think how other faithful believers live out God's truth. Consider what may keep you from living the truth out yourself. As you sense your inability to live out some truth, come before God humbly and silently. See clearly how incapable you are. Ask God to live His life in you and to do for you all that you cannot do yourself. He will certainly finish the work that He started in you.[21]

Coming To Grips

If it hasn't sunk in yet, here it is. Let's face it; we are our own worst enemy. We always want things our way, and we often lose the fight to create unity due to our lack of self-awareness and care for others. James 4:1-3 says:

> ¹ What causes quarrels and what causes fights among you? Is it not this, that your passions are at war within you? ² You desire and do not have, so you murder. You covet and cannot obtain, so you fight and quarrel. You do not have, because you do not ask. ³ You ask and do not receive, because you ask wrongly, to spend it on your passions.

James presents two questions to his readers. And even though the second seems to answer the first, he explains in further detail the root cause of fights and quarrels among believers. What hinders unity? The short answer is sin. But what sins in particular? James tells us that the issues are our evil desires, covetousness, and misguided prayers. Author Paul Cedar wrote the following:

> James begins his teaching regarding the conflict of pride and prayer by posing an important question, "Where do wars and fights come from among you?" The basic assumption is that such conflicts are taking place within the interpersonal relationships of his readers.

The word James uses for "war" is pólemos, which means just that: war or battle. The word translated as "fights" is máchē which can also be correctly translated as strife, struggles, or quarrelings. To be sure, both of these words denote interpersonal conflicts. James not only poses the question; he gives a very graphic and appropriate answer. Simply stated, we are involved in conflicts because of our desires for pleasure or lusts that are in conflict within our very selves. We are at war inwardly so it is natural for us to be at war outwardly.[22]

Evil Desires

The first issue that James presents is that our relational problems do not stem from upholding the truth nor from our righteous anger. Instead, it is our desires that find their source from our self-indulgence. James is simply reinforcing what the Apostle Paul has already told us in Galatians 5, that the Spirit and the flesh are at war. James wants us to understand that when we allow the flesh (our irritations, pride, crookedness, and evil plots) to be victorious within us, the only natural outcome is to be at war with others. When we lack personal growth in our relationship with Jesus, we will not foster Kingdom relationships with others. And when we put our sinful desires over God's kingdom, we intentionally and unintentionally tear others down for the sole benefit of our interests. Within all of us, evil lusts of all kinds can cause us to take our eyes off of what God has called us to do and will lead us to focus solely on ourselves. This causes spiritual blindness and leads us to live independently of God and how He requires us to love one another.

The Coveting Problem

The next issue James gives us is that we covet. And for many of us, we covet one thing that only God has: control! Too often, we want to be in control of our lives and the lives of others. However, we don't control time, we don't control how and when we are born, we don't control the color of our skin, we don't control people or what happens to us or around us, and yet we still try to be in control of everything. God alone is sovereign. The problem is that we often want to act like the Holy Spirit, meaning we want to be God and be in control of not only our own lives but also the lives of others.

We somehow believe that we are the fourth person in the Trinity. We want to control what other people think and how they live. We want to tell them what to think so long as it makes us happy. We want to tell them how to vote, what to watch, and how to feel. Some of us unconsciously guilt and manipulate people to live as we live. Whatever we prescribe to ourselves for our spiritual journey, we enforce that prescription on others, whether they know it or not. For example, if we don't watch certain movies, others should not watch the same movies. After giving our prescription, the true intention of our hearts is revealed when they ignore us.

What happens? When people decide not to heed our so-called wisdom and refuse our control, we get upset and wonder how they are even Christians. Our negative response exposes how we genuinely desire to control them and play the role of God in their lives, even if we think it is for their good.

Misguided Prayer

One of the demands of being a disciple of Jesus is that our prayers line up with His will. This leads us to the third issue that causes division in the church: misguided prayers. Our prayers will be flawed when our soul is defiled, we delight in division, or we desire to control others. When we spend more time praying for other people to be "fixed" and for others to see things the way we see them, we assume that we are 100% right. The truth is that we are only right if our desires align with God's will. It is not God's will for His children to be Democrat or Republican. I do not believe it is God's will for us to be divided theologically. It is not God's will that everyone is a part of a secular movement or agrees with it wholeheartedly.

It is God's will that His children obey Him above all things. God's will is for His people to be just, merciful, and humble. Our perspective on life and our prayers need to change. Instead of praying that other Christians see things the way we see them, we should ask God to give us the patience to love them, give us the ability to serve them and change our hearts to see them the way He sees them. Instead of praying against the government, its leaders, civil rights activists, and others, we should thank God for them, praying that they lead with wisdom and that God would bring blessings out of them.

We should be praying that all followers of Jesus grow in the knowledge of Him and His grace. Even if we believe that others are the enemy, God tells us to love them (Matthew 5:44). If others mistreat us, we are told to pray for them and extend grace. We are to go the extra mile in our love for them. This is what the Father has done with us and what He calls us to do with others.

Knowing that spiritual swamps exist, the goal is to be transformed into Christ-likeness. To do this, we must love. But the question we must answer is, "Are we willing to embrace a love that submits itself to others for their betterment?" Loving others and praying for others like this is the pathway to unity and continual death of self. Let's take a look at the path we must follow.

The Denied Life

We are called to devote our lives to having the same love for others that Christ has for us. To achieve this, we must not let our selfishness get in the way of what God is trying to do in and through us. Here are some examples of a selfish mindset:

1. When decisions are made, I only think of myself.
2. I only think about my common interests, and I disregard the interests of others.
3. I promote my interests and purpose.
4. My self-worth is based on how I perform for people.
5. I want people to serve me.
6. I can control my surroundings and other people.
7. I want to be approved and loved by all people.
8. I fear being rejected by others, so I will hurt them because they have hurt me.
9. I don't rejoice when others are blessed.
10. I take rather than give

11. Submitting to God's will is very difficult because I genuinely want to live my life.
12. I believe I am better than anyone who is not like me.

These 12 pillars of selfishness are just a tiny example, yet Jesus still tells us to deny ourselves. His remedy to these 12 statements is listed below.

1. Consider how your decisions will impact others. (1 Corinthians 10:24)
2. Take time to consider the needs of other people. (Philippians 2:4)
3. Proclaim the Kingdom of God. (Matthew 28:19)
4. You don't have to perform for God. You have been accepted because of Jesus' work on the cross. (Romans 5:1, 2 Corinthians 5:21)
5. Serve others. (Matthew 20:26-28)
6. Surrender to the Lord; He holds all power. (John 15:5)
7. God has approved of you. (Galatians 1:10, 1 John 3:1)
8. Walk in peace with others. (Romans 12:17-18)
9. Celebrate the success of others. (Romans 12:15)
10. Give generously. (2 Corinthians 9:6)
11. Your life is not about you. (Luke 22:42, Galatians 2:20)
12. Acknowledge that you still sin, and sometimes you do it a lot. (1 John 1:8-10)

Author and counselor Lou Priolo once wrote, "Never lose sight of the fact that selfishness is the one sin out of which all others flow. To mortify selfishness is to subdue the chief enemy of your soul. It is to remove from the Devil the greatest handle by which he attempts to influence and seduce us."[23] When we deny our natural tendencies and supernaturally stand as one, via the power of the Holy Spirit, we show the world that one of the things that demonstrates the reign of God and brings the Father joy is when His children live as one and embrace their differences. In my journey, I believe that to destroy the Me Monster within us, we have to focus on at least four things.

Surrender of Rights

Too often, as Christ-followers, we believe we are owed certain rights. We think the kingdom of God operates like the American government. We grow up being told things like, "Live your best life," and then we take all of those rights and pride and try to transfer those same things into God's kingdom. We fall into the trap of thinking that we still have the right to life, liberty, and the pursuit of happiness in Christ. But the rights of America are in direct contradiction to God's kingdom. Instead of the right to live, we are responsible for dying to ourselves. Instead of our right to liberty, we are called to be slaves to righteousness. Instead of pursuing happiness, we must pursue holiness. As Christians, our lives are not our own. When we said yes to Jesus, we surrendered all of our rights to God, and they have been replaced with kingdom responsibilities. We are called to live up to our foremost responsibility and duty, representing Jesus in life.

Embrace The Duty to Love

Defaulting to self-preservation comes naturally to us all. This trait can be seen even in the most sincere of Christians. God desires that we do not just love people but embrace our duty to love. We must love even when we don't feel like loving. We must love even when the love is not being reciprocated. Love is not something the Father has requested of us; it is something He requires of us. The duty to love is to pick up the cross so that others can experience the righteousness of God.

Live out our Godly Responsibility

Ephesians 5:20-21 says, "giving thanks always and for everything to God the Father in the name of our Lord Jesus Christ, submitting to one another out of reverence for Christ." Although our rights may seem significant, what is of greater importance is that we mutually submit to one another. Our responsibility is to treat each other as equals even when we risk being taken advantage of. The goal is for us to love our neighbors and not oppress them.

Be Focused on the Mission

Satan is always trying to keep believers apart because he knows how dangerous we would be if we walked in unity. As believers, we are called to love God, love our enemy, make disciples, and be one. However, distractions attempt to keep us from doing that. Author and speaker Bob Goff once said, "Satan only needs to distract us and not destroy us."[24] When we are distracted, we lose focus. And when we lose focus, we lose purpose. Paul urges us in the first three verses of Colossians 3 to keep our minds on things in heaven above and not on earth below because if we maintain throne-room thinking, we would be focused on God's purpose and not our preferences. Throne-room thinking keeps our attention on the mission God has for us and silences distractions. If we are going to get out of our spiritual swamps, we must have throne-room thinking because it leads to redemptive behaviors. When we move away from a swamp mentality to a kingdom mentality, we will see progress in the church when it comes to being unified.

Killing the Me Monster

The battle against the Me Monster is a spiritual journey of self-awareness. It is the recognition that we all can lurk in the swamps of self-trust and self-preservation. To overcome these internal foes, we must embrace our responsibilities of surrendering our rights for the sake of others, love others sacrificially, resist the temptation to oppress or discriminate against people, and silence distractions that hinder us along the way. When we acknowledge our Me Monster, we pave the way for unity to begin in the body of Christ. As we are vigilant in this inner battle, we will destroy the Me Monster and become instruments of unity in a divided church.

5

Focused on God's Glory

> *Worthy are you, our Lord and God, to receive glory and honor and power, for you created all things, and by your will they existed and were created.* — **Revelation 4:11**

It was the summer of 2010, and my wife was pregnant with our first child. We were both super excited and highly terrified about having children. After reading parenting books and talking to other parents with kids, we knew it would be a rewarding experience but also challenging. We had high anticipation, but the thought of losing sleep because of a newborn tempered our excitement. Amid all the emotions, we were still prepared, maybe overprepared, for the future arrival of our daughter. I had repainted the room for our coming princess, and my wife started buying everything necessary to baby-proof the house.

We were doing all we could to prepare for the October delivery day. That all changed in July. My wife had scheduled a routine pregnancy appointment, and after that, we planned on going to a wedding reception. On the way to the appointment, we discussed what we would wear to the reception and how we probably would not stay long. It was a nice summer day in Philadelphia, and we did not live too far from the doctor's office, which was also at the hospital where my wife would give birth to our first child in a few months.

We had taken this drive many times and discussed how fast I would drive once she went into labor. Shortly after arriving at the doctor's office, my wife was told she had a lot of protein in her urine. She was instructed to go to triage so they could run further tests. Doctors ran more tests in triage and took her blood pressure, which was very high and rapidly rising. They gave her medicine to decrease her blood pressure, but nothing changed. As I sat in the room with my wife, the doctor told us she was suffering from preeclampsia. After explaining preeclampsia, he said the baby would have to be delivered that day. The options he gave us were:

> Option #1. Have the surgery, and both mom and baby may live.
>
> Option #2. Have the surgery, and either mom or baby will live.
>
> Option #3. Don't have the surgery, and mom and baby will die.

No brainer, right? Without hesitation, we opted for the surgery. And just like that, the joy of my wife experiencing a full-term pregnancy, going into labor and speeding to the hospital while telling her to breathe was gone. They rushed her to the operating room and told me I had to wait outside. Frightened and frustrated, I waited outside the operating room, thinking about a future without one or both of my girls. I decided to call my pastor, and he and some of the church members came to the hospital, sat in the waiting room, and prayed for us.

As I sat and waited, I remember praying in faith and desperation. "Lord, if only one comes out, neither of them comes out, or both come out, You are still good." It was probably one of the most honest prayers I have ever prayed. And as I waited, I decided to see some of my church family praying for us in the waiting room. When I saw them, one of the sisters asked if my wife, Tiffanie, and the baby would be okay. My only response was, "I don't know. I pray that God is glorified." In one of the most stressful moments, my only concern was that God would be glorified, no matter the outcome. All I knew was that God was good and would work it out.

Shortly after, the doctor told me the surgery was successful and that my wife and newborn daughter were alive. As I walked into the operating room, I saw the miracle. My daughter, Imani (Swahili for Faith), was born 1 lb 12 oz. As I held her in the palm of my hand, I saw how tiny she was, and my only thought was, "Thank you, Lord." Later on, I saw my wife. She battled through the surgery and was wondering if all had gone well. I told her everything was good and told her to rest. Again, my only thought was, "Thank you, Lord."

After seeing my wife, the doctor told me my daughter was not in the clear just yet. As it turned out, Imani would have to spend the next three months in the NICU (neonatal intensive care unit), where babies get around-the-clock care. My wife and I went to see her every day. And we prayed for her every day and thanked God for what He was doing. I would sit there, singing songs to her while at the same time looking at her tiny body with small plastic tubes in her nose. Day after day, my wife and I continued to deal with uncertainty, and yet, through prayer, there was one thing I could lean on: the goodness and glory of the Lord.

As we stand toe-to-toe with the world seeking unity and when we are about to go through or are in suffering, the prayers we pray at those crucial times genuinely reveal who we are. Those kinds of prayers show the actual condition of our hearts, whom we trust, and whom we glorify. The same can be said about Jesus. In the gospel of John, right before Jesus is about to be arrested (the beginning of suffering), He prays what has been called "The High Priestly Prayer." And in His prayer in John 17:1, He begins by saying, "Father, the hour has come; glorify your Son that the Son may glorify you."

For Jesus, the glory of the Father was critical and foundational regardless of what He was going through. He had a value system where His top priority was the Father receiving glory. Jesus understood that everything, every crisis, every significant emotional event, every discomfort, and every success begins and ends with the glory of God. As the prayer started, Jesus practiced the art of keeping the main thing the main thing: giving God glory even as He approached the cross.

Giving God Glory

As you read throughout scripture, you will see a common theme of how God's primary concern is to be glorified. This revelation leads us to understand how seriously God desires to see His creation worship Him and Him alone. In Exodus 14:4, as God is talking about Pharoah, He says, "And I will harden Pharaoh's heart, and he will pursue them, and I will get **glory** over Pharaoh and all his host, and the Egyptians shall know that I am the Lord." Pharaoh honestly thought that he was a god, and while trying to exert his power over the Israelites, God was still going to be glorified by showing Pharoah and his army that He was superior. That also meant killing the firstborn son of a self-proclaimed god-king. Here are some additional passages in the Bible that speak to glorifying God:

1 Chronicles 16:24
Declare his **glory** among the nations, his marvelous works among all the peoples!

Psalm 57:5
Be exalted, O God, above the heavens! Let your **glory** be over all the earth!

Matthew 5:16
In the same way, let your light shine before others, so that they may see your good works and give **glory** to your Father who is in heaven

Romans 11:36
For from him and through him and to him are all things. To him be **glory** forever. Amen.

1 Corinthians 10:31
So, whether you eat or drink, or whatever you do, do all to the **glory** of God.

The glory of God is not something that we can simply gloss over. Scripture is laced with references regarding God's desire to be glorified, especially amongst His creation. Psalm 145:9-13 says:

> [9] The Lord is good to all, and his mercy is over all that he has made. [10] All your works shall give thanks to you, O Lord, and all your saints shall bless you! [11] They shall speak of the **glory** of your kingdom and tell of your power, [12] to make known to the children of man your mighty deeds, and the **glorious** splendor of your kingdom. [13] Your kingdom is an everlasting kingdom, and your dominion endures throughout all generations

God's glory is also connected with His immensity and His kingdom. God and His character are attached to his glory. To not recognize this or ignore that God desires to be glorified in all we do and not be in awe of God and His nature is detrimental. When we are no longer in awe of God, eventually, we will not respect God, and if we don't respect God, we will naturally disrespect His creation, including people who are made in His image and likeness. In addition, we will eventually begin to give His glory to something else. Romans 1:22-25 says:

> "Claiming to be wise, they became fools and exchanged the glory of the immortal God for images resembling mortal man and birds and animals and creeping things. Therefore God gave them up in the lusts of their hearts to impurity, to the dishonoring of their bodies among themselves, because they exchanged the truth about God for a

> lie and worshiped and served the creature rather than the Creator, who is blessed forever! Amen."

These verses sum up the plight of humanity. Absolute truth is wrapped up in God's glory. When we disregard the truth, we refuse to glorify God. We also refuse to glorify God when we worship and glorify the created instead of the Creator. This compromise of the faith is not just reflected in the New Testament. In the Old Testament book of Zephaniah 1:4-6 (NIV), we read:

> "I will stretch out my hand against Judah and against all who live in Jerusalem. I will destroy every remnant of Baal worship in this place, the very names of the idolatrous priests - those who bow down on the roofs to worship the starry host, those who bow down and swear by the Lord and who also swear by Molek, those who turn back from following the Lord and neither seek the Lord nor inquire of him."

God's judgment comes against His people because they worshiped Him and bowed to other gods. This violates Exodus 20:3, "Do not have other gods besides me." In the Old Testament, we see the worship of God and Baal. There is the worship of God and starry hosts (celestial gods, moon god, sun god). Then there is the worship of God and the Canaanite god Molek. Many believed that if they sacrificed their children to Molek, they would prosper, and their future children would prosper. For the nation of Israel, worshipping God alone was insufficient. They wanted a "side god."

Not much has changed today. Too often, because of our human condition, we tend to accept a theology of delusion where we embrace syncretism. A basic definition of syncretism is the blending of religions, cultures, or philosophies. For example, sometimes, we fuse too much of the world with our Christianity, leading us to place our faith in Jesus and *something else*. It can be Jesus and white nationalism. Jesus and socialism. Jesus and politics. Jesus and black consciousness. Jesus and astrology. Jesus and Western culture.

This deception will only continue to knit our hearts and conform our minds to this world. And though we may feel we are living the way God intends for us to live, we are being swallowed up through syncretism. This leads to division, which causes many believers to be hurt by the church and many non-believers to be turned away from the faith. This delusional Christianity dilutes the gospel and takes glory away from the Father.

Embracing and worshipping Jesus and _____ says to the Father, "Jesus is not enough." But Jesus is, in fact, enough. When we do not embrace and worship Jesus alone, it weakens the witness of our oneness and makes oneness in the church harder to achieve. If we can shatter the walls of syncretism, we will see the glory of God manifested in the beauty of our diversity and the power of our oneness.

Glorify God Through the Gospel

In the high priestly prayer of Jesus, he goes on to pray that followers of Christ be one. Our oneness, albeit uncomfortable at times, should be a byproduct of glorifying God. When God's glory is no longer the top priority in our lives, we will inevitably prioritize the irrelevant things of this world. The result is that we produce an incendiary sense of ego, superiority, and narrow-mindedness.

As a result, harmony and peace within the church (both local and universal) become very difficult and almost impossible to achieve because self-centeredness, racism, colorism, politics, economics, and other things become a part of what we worship. It is impossible to experience an authentic, loving, and unified community when our identities are wholly tethered to created things and not the Creator. As image-bearers of God, we are responsible for recognizing God's sovereignty and responding to Him in a way that exalts Him alone.

Galatians 3:28 says, "There is neither Jew nor Greek, there is neither slave nor free, there is no male and female, for you are all one in Christ

Jesus." Because of Jesus, **ALL** are welcome. God wants a world where diverse people are submitted and united with Him and each other yet still peacefully distinct. This is the beauty of the gospel.

Through the death and resurrection of Jesus, there can be peace between **ALL** people groups. And though there are distinctions in these groups, these differences are to be embraced, and at the same time, they are to be radically subordinate to the authority of God. Though they are to be celebrated, the things that make us distinct no longer separate us. This new identity in Christ further proves to the world that the gospel is powerful enough to forgive sins, reconcile us to God, and unify those who were at one point living in disunity.

The enemy has tried to distort the gospel and has misled many to embrace secular social constructs to dupe them into thinking that even after salvation, one group is superior to the other. We are tricked into embracing other tribes within Christendom, whether it be a political, ethnic, or doctrinal tribe. And we dismiss or want to "cancel" anyone unlike us. Yet, the truth is that none of us are righteous on our own, and we are one people submitted to God in Christ. When we embrace this truth, we glorify the Creator over the created.

Because of the gospel, we should intentionally create unity in the church. If we do not see the need to be one and live in unity as believers in Christ, then we suffer from spiritual blindness. It is through this blindness that we will create more division and harm others in the body of Christ. What results from this rebellion is that we disregard God's glory.

Now, I know that some would say, "Just get saved, then we are all one, and everything will be okay. It will all work out." I believe this is a half-truth. Based on Jesus' prayer in John, 17, there is biblical evidence of the kingdom's mandate for an intentional effort to be put toward unification in the body of Christ. Our oneness is the will of God and we must put forth effort to live in obedience to His will. When we also examine Ephesians 2, we see it clearly explained by the Apostle Paul:

> [1] "And you were dead in the trespasses and sins [2] in which you once walked, following the course of this world, following the prince of the power of the air, the spirit that is now at work in the sons of disobedience— [3] among whom we all once lived in the passions of our flesh, carrying out the desires of the body and the mind, and were by nature children of wrath, like the rest of mankind. [4] But God, being rich in mercy, because of the great love with which he loved us, [5] even when we were dead in our trespasses, made us alive together with Christ—by grace you have been saved— [6] and raised us up with him and seated us with him in the heavenly places in Christ Jesus, [7] so that in the coming ages he might show the immeasurable riches of his grace in kindness toward us in Christ Jesus. [8] For by grace you have been saved through faith. And this is not your own doing; it is the gift of God, [9] not a result of works, so that no one may boast. [10] For we are his workmanship, created in Christ Jesus for good works, which God prepared beforehand, that we should walk in them...."

The condition of humanity is naturally divisive, disobedient, and depraved because this is the way of the world. We are all made in the image of God, but because of the fall in Genesis, we are equally human, and we are equally broken and equally in need of a Savior. Because God is rich in mercy and loves us, He made us alive together with Christ and has prepared good works for us to do (Eph 2:8-10). And one of the good works after receiving the good news of Jesus is that we work to live as one in Christ.

This is indeed good news, but it is also work that must be done intentionally. The second half of Ephesians 2 says:

> [11] Therefore remember that at one time you Gentiles in the flesh, called "the uncircumcision" by what is called the circumcision, which is made in the flesh by hands— [12] remember that you were at that time separated from Christ, alienated from the commonwealth

of Israel and strangers to the covenants of promise, having no hope and without God in the world. [13] But now in Christ Jesus you who once were far off have been brought near by the blood of Christ. [14] For he himself is our peace, who has made us both one and has broken down in his flesh the dividing wall of hostility [15] by abolishing the law of commandments expressed in ordinances, that he might create in himself one new man in place of the two, so making peace, [16] and might reconcile us both to God in one body through the cross, thereby killing the hostility. [17] And he came and preached peace to you who were far off and peace to those who were near. [18] For through him we both have access in one Spirit to the Father. [19] So then you are no longer strangers and aliens, but you are fellow citizens with the saints and members of the household of God, [20] built on the foundation of the apostles and prophets, Christ Jesus himself being the cornerstone, [21] in whom the whole structure, being joined together, grows into a holy temple in the Lord. [22] In him you also are being built together into a dwelling place for God by the Spirit.

The power of the gospel is that it not only redeems and justifies us, it also reconciles us to one another. This glorifies the Father. The ability to peacefully agree to disagree and still walk in harmony (without bitterness or resentment) is good work for the world to see. This glorifies the Father. Matthew 5:16 says, "In the same way, let your light shine before others, so that they may see your good works and give glory to your Father who is in heaven." Good works glorify the Father, which is the main thing we must always keep in mind. God's glory and not our own should always be our primary concern.

Two Brothers

In 2017, according to a Reuters survey, racism and bigotry in the U.S. posed an imminent threat to the country. During this time, my family and I relocated from Texas and started serving at Sandhills

PEOPLE SUCK, GOD IS GOOD

Community Church in Columbia, SC. Jeff, the senior pastor (who is white), and I clicked immediately. We talked about racial reconciliation and injustice when I first came on staff. He shared with me his passion for racial reconciliation in the church.

He told me he was a fan of Dr. John Perkins and spent time with Dr. Perkins. Jeff was excited to have a black pastor on staff again, but more than that, he had a black pastor on staff seeking ethnic unification in the church. Don't get me wrong; Jeff likes to work on cars, is a fan of Disney movies, and likes the Kansas City Chiefs. I like to drive cars, like Disney Marvel movies, and like the Philadelphia Eagles. We are very different. However, the beauty of our friendship is that we embrace how we are different and use those differences to improve each other.

During my first year at the church, I remember how refreshing it was to go on a double date with our wives and interact with them. I can honestly say that they have a firm grasp of what the church should be and were living it out. Then, in January 2018, Jeff asked me to preach with him on the subject of unity. We talked about it, lamented over the state of the world, the country, the state, and the church, looked at scripture, and prepared as best we could. Then, on that Sunday, January 21, 2018, we preached about ethnic unity in the church. We were laughing and just being ourselves during the sermon. We did not pull any punches as we acknowledged the ethnic tensions, political differences, and other silos inside the church. And as we spoke, we pointed out that not all people are bigots or sexist. It could be that people can just be jerks.

After the sermon, something very impactful happened. People began to comment that what impacted them the most was seeing two men (one black and one white) together, sharing the word of God, and demonstrating a genuine love for one another. It was awesome to hear that the two of us preaching together and having an authentic friendship demonstrated God's greatness. By preaching together, we have realized that our physical presence together in the pulpit and love for one another spoke to the hearts of the people who long to see unity in the church or who may be struggling with the issues that prevent harmony in the church.

Since then, Jeff and I have co-preached and co-taught in the church, Christian workshops, university classrooms, and corporate conferences. He and I have developed a relationship where we can look at each other and know what we are thinking. We don't just have a Sunday relationship. So when people see us together and serving together, they see what God can do with two people who are completely different, completely surrendered to the Lord, and want to see unity in the lives of all people, especially those in the church.

The Father wants us to be one. But as His children, if we never fully surrender to the greatness of God in every aspect of life, never cultivate godly relationships with people not like us, and remain loyal to things other than God, we will not experience divine transformation or true fellowship with others. This is a massive undertaking as Christians because we are so tethered to the world and have made idols out of so many things. The voice of John can be heard even clearer when he says in 1 John 5:21, "Little children, keep yourselves from idols."

Connectivity to the world prohibits us as God's children from living out the high priestly prayer of Jesus in John 17. We cannot be extensions of divine oneness and fully glorify God if we do not surrender our stereotypes, prejudices, bigotry, ethnocentrism, theology, and worldview to God. To be one means there is suffering, service, and steadfastness involved. (More about that later.)

These selfless acts call us to surrender our rights and live up to our sacred responsibility to have true fellowship with other believers. So, to achieve unity and not just uniformity, there must be a spiritual transformation that begins by accepting the revelation that God is glorified when we live as one in the body of Christ. Dr. Tony Evans wrote:

> The goal of the church should be to glorify God by reflecting the values of God among the people of God through letting the truth of God be the standard by which we measure right and wrong and the

way we accept skin color, class and culture...God is a God of multi-coloredness. God loves the variety in His garden called earth, and each one of us has equal value; after all, He died for each one."[25]

Keep the Main Thing The Main Thing

The idea of keeping the main thing the main thing has often been used as a cop-out in conversations to avoid the issues we contend with. One may say, "Let's just worship Jesus, and everything will be okay." Unfortunately, this type of theology is in error because if one tries to avoid confronting sin, specifically disunity, their worship is not in Spirit and Truth. How can we truly worship God and never fully address the issues plaguing other members of Christ that lead to division and brokenness in the church?

Isaiah 1:11-18 gives us a primer for what God wants from His people.

> [11] "What to me is the multitude of your sacrifices? says the Lord; I have had enough of burnt offerings of rams and the fat of well-fed beasts; I do not delight in the blood of bulls, or of lambs, or goats. [12] "When you come to appear before me, who has required of you this trampling of my courts? [13] Bring no more vain offerings; incense is an abomination to me. New moon and Sabbath and the calling of convocations— I cannot endure iniquity and solemn assembly. [14] Your new moons and your appointed feasts my soul hates; they have become a burden to me; I am weary of bearing them. [15] When you spread out your hands, I will hide my eyes from you; even though you make many prayers, I will not listen; your hands are full of blood. [16] Wash yourselves; make yourselves clean; remove the evil of your deeds from before my eyes; cease to do evil, [17] learn to do good; seek justice, correct oppression; bring justice to the fatherless, plead the widow's cause. [18] "Come now, let us reason together, says the Lord: though your sins are like scarlet, they shall be as white as snow; though they are red like crimson, they shall become like wool. [19] If you are willing and obedient, you shall eat the good of the land; [20]

but if you refuse and rebel, you shall be eaten by the sword; for the mouth of the Lord has spoken."

Keeping the main thing the main thing means that we will not use the worship of God or theology to avoid issues that lead to disunity but that we are willing to address these issues or begin to learn about them to address them in the future because that honors God and is true worship.

In verse 17, the Lord explicitly states that they must **learn to do good** and **correct oppression.** Learning or making ourselves accustomed to the struggles of others delights the Father. Because when our hearts break and grieve over the sin and struggle of others, then we will demonstrate more compassion for others and a desire to make things right. If we refuse to make things right and continue in our divisive ways, the text clearly says that God will hide His eyes from us. We cannot wash ourselves of sin; Jesus does that. However, there are two things we can do that will put us on the path of unification and glorification of the Father.

Glorify God Through Forgiveness

In 1999, after graduating from college, I moved to Norcross, GA, outside Atlanta. I was a manager trainee working for a credit card organization and had ambitions of climbing the corporate ladder. During my time there, I met another trainee "Jay." At that time, Jay was the stereotypical American white guy. He had a solid education, came from affluence, and flaunted it.

Jay and I never got along. It's possible we felt threatened by each other. One evening, as Jay and I were in the office, he demanded some data and that I call a client. I was shocked because I did not report to him. Like me, he was a trainee, yet the way he ordered me around at that moment rubbed me the wrong way. It hurt because he took a superior posture over me when he had no justification for doing so.

My response was simple, "Get it yourself. I am not your house nigger." Jay looked at me with shock. In his mind, he did nothing wrong. He gave me the "Are you calling me a racist?" look. After that event, I never spoke to Jay again. But every time we passed each other in the office, I looked at him with hatred, and he shared the same look. In my mind, extending forgiveness to Jay was not, nor would it ever be an option. He never apologized for crossing the line and not treating me as his peer. And I am not sure I would have forgiven him, even if he did apologize.

Thinking about that season of my life, I have learned firsthand that maybe one of the hardest parts of the Christian faith is extending forgiveness to those who have hurt me. In the past, when I dealt with anyone like Jay, I put them into the "white people suck" category in my brain. Once they fell into that category, the last thing I wanted to do was forgive them. The problem is that mentally holding people in this category eventually seeped into my heart, resulting in growing bitterness and hatred toward white people.

In hindsight, the root of the issue was that I felt disrespected, and my ego was crushed. I projected onto Jay all of my hurt from racism in the past that I had not dealt with. Today, I realize that some of my selfish responses to people I knew or thought were racist, especially Jay, may have been based on the fact that I had not processed my own negative racial experiences in the past. My default explanation when someone white mistreated me was that they had to be racist.

I had not dealt with my previous painful experiences and was not mature enough to identify the enemy's tricks and see that my identity is wrapped up in Jesus, not in someone who thinks or acts like they are better than me. Don't get me wrong; some people behave in racially motivated ways. However, I know now that some people are not being racist. They are just mean. And that's putting it softly.

So here is a question for you: Who is God calling you to forgive for the sake of unity so that God would be glorified? When we forgive others who have wronged us, we give people a glimpse of the gospel.

In his book, "The Relationship Principles of Jesus," Tom Holladay wrote, "Selfishness must be replaced by unselfishness. Conceit must be replaced with compassion and ego must be replaced with altruism. The focus on "me" must give way to "we." It's all about loving God and others."[26]

The radical aspect of the gospel is that it crashes into our cultures, and it hurts. And by the power of the Holy Spirit, it challenges us to forgive others even if there is never any confession of sin. For example, Jesus stated in Luke 23:34, "Father, forgive them, for they know not what they do." As a form of intercession, Jesus cried out to the Father for Him to forgive the people and the guards who had not asked for forgiveness, nor did they think they had done anything wrong.

From this, we see that compassion, grace, and forgiveness are at the core of Christ's heart. Though confession from the offender is the desired outcome when it comes to forgiving others, we can conclude, from the plea of Jesus, that we are called to forgive even when confession is absent or the offender is clueless that an offense has been committed. We must learn how to develop hearts of forgiveness, especially when dealing with people who have wronged us and think they have good intentions. Though it is difficult to do, having a heart of forgiveness includes praying for the welfare of those who have offended us, serving those who have offended us, sacrificing for those who have offended us, and ultimately loving those who have offended us by not holding their offense against them. John Perkins echoed this when he said:

> "The ability to forgive is made possible by the power of the Holy Spirit who indwells the heart of every believer. But that does not mean it is easy....to forgive is to make a decision to cancel a debt that you are owed and not hold it against your offender. There is no forgiveness with a debt."[27]

When we forgive, we absorb the offender's fault and endure the pain that comes with forgiveness. Forgiveness is the capital that drives the gospel economy. It drives away anger and gives hope to others. By extending forgiveness to others, we are presenting to them the love God has shown us, hoping their hearts will change. Again, in Luke 23:34, Jesus said, "Father forgive them for they know not what they do."[28] After he extended forgiveness, let's examine what ensues in verses 46-47.

> [46] Then Jesus, calling out with a loud voice, said, "Father, into your hands I commit my spirit!" And having said this he breathed his last. [47] Now when the centurion saw what had taken place, he praised God, saying, "Certainly this man was innocent!"

Within the context of these verses, we are introduced to a Roman officer overseeing Jesus's crucifixion. This profound act of forgiveness demonstrated by Jesus impacted the officer so much that he praised God, which was uncommon for Romans at that time. Jesus' forgiveness changed his heart. For us, having a heart of forgiveness is a game-changer for unity because there is more potential for believing and unbelieving hearts to change, which further glorifies God and leads us further down the path of unity.

Glorify God Through Confession

My wife has loved me for over 17 years. She has been and continues to be my rock. Listening is one of her best skills, and I often think she is a silent assassin because she is so attentive to what people say as they talk to her. But she is also skilled at calling me out when I mess up. One morning, she was trying to sleep in, and I got up early and started cleaning up. I thought I was doing a great job by taking on this chore so she would not feel like she had to give up rest to clean up around the house.

My thinking was all wrong. As I played the music downstairs, it woke her up, and when I went upstairs, she asked me what I was doing in a sassy tone. With a smile on my face, I told her that I was cleaning up. She looked perplexed. She did not say thank you. She talked about how loud the music was and that she was trying to sleep. In my defense, I told her that I was doing it for her. She looked at me with the "you know you are wrong" look. I had an attitude as I went back downstairs. This is where the story gets interesting.

While downstairs, I started having a conversation with myself. "What did I do wrong? I didn't do anything wrong. Was I wrong? I need to confess that I offended her. But why confess if I did not do anything wrong? Wait...she needs to confess to me. I am offended. I was trying to help her out. I am not confessing a thing. I'm a grown man. How can she talk to me like that? Wait...was I wrong?"

After several minutes of being angry and conversing with myself, I could hear the Holy Spirit saying, "Go and confess that you offended her and that you are sorry for the miscommunication." After standing in the kitchen debating whether I should go back upstairs to confess my offense, I finally went. It was so humbling because I thought I was right. It was hard because I thought I was helping.

As I approached the bedroom, in my humble voice, I said, "Babe, I'm sorry for waking you up and not communicating what I was trying to do. Please forgive me." Her demeanor immediately changed. Not only did she forgive me, but she also asked that I forgive her for not saying thank you and getting so upset with me. Confession of my offense changed her heart toward me and brought reconciliation between us.

We have discussed the importance of forgiveness and how it can profoundly impact those who have committed an offense against us. Confession also has a tremendous impact on people. When we sin, we do so against God, but frequently against someone else. The prodigal son said in Luke 15:21, "Father, I have sinned against heaven and before you...." Confessing our sins one to another can significantly impact how we relate to each other. The problem is that too often, confession never happens, which leads to the continuation of broken relationships.

Let's be honest. Confession of sin is problematic because it rubs against all of our pride. And with pride being one of the most brutal sins to overcome, we will always find it challenging to snitch on ourselves.

As fallen beings, we tend to think highly of ourselves and assume that our behaviors and motives are pure. Just ask everyone who took part in the crucifixion of Jesus. They thought they were doing the right thing. So even in our efforts to please God, the most committed Christians will find themselves doing or saying something moronic and perhaps motivated by selfishness.

We deceive ourselves into thinking we are better than we are, and when we recognize (*if* we recognize) that we have sinned, an internal battle occurs within us. Do I confess or don't I? After all, some of us believe that confession makes us look weak; for others, it makes them feel like they have compromised who they are. We try to reason with our pride and justify our actions to avoid being humbled in the presence of others. So we often take the cheap road and build our lives and other relationships on unconfessed sin or an escapist confession (I apologize *if* I offended you) and then wonder why some of our relationships are not what they should be.

In any discussion about unity, I believe we all need to confess something. Some of us need to confess past or present actions, and others need to confess past or present attitudes. The church is in a divisive crisis where confession must happen for restoration to begin. In the Old Testament book of Nehemiah chapter one, we find Jerusalem in a crisis condition:

> ⁴ As soon as I heard these words I sat down and wept and mourned for days, and I continued fasting and praying before the God of heaven. ⁵ And I said, "O Lord God of heaven, the great and awesome God who keeps covenant and steadfast love with those who love him and keep his commandments, ⁶ let your ear be attentive and your eyes open, to hear the prayer of your servant that I now pray before you day and night for the people of Israel your servants, confessing the sins of the people of Israel, which we have sinned against you. Even I and my father's house have sinned.

> ⁷ We have acted very corruptly against you and have not kept the commandments, the statutes, and the rules that you commanded your servant Moses.

The report given to Nehemiah is that the Jews have survived exile but are not enjoying or taking advantage of their freedom; instead, they are in great distress. Some would even argue that the Jews at this time were living in shame as they faced potential threats and calamities. There is also an issue with the city. The Bible says that the walls of Jerusalem are broken down, and its gates are burned with fire. The news about Jerusalem catches Nehemiah by surprise.

Nehemiah is deeply distressed about the state of Jerusalem. And during his season of lament, he goes into a season of confession. In Nehemiah 1:6, he confesses using the term "we" and not just "I" or "they." He lumps himself in with the people and not only confesses those sins, but he continues to confess the sins of his forefathers. Nehemiah 1:7 says, "We have acted very corruptly against you and have not kept the commandments, the statutes, and the rules that you commanded your servant Moses."

They have all been guilty to a certain degree, and Nehemiah understands that the current situation can't be put on one group of people. Therefore, he includes himself as one who has also sinned. "Note that Nehemiah identifies with a generation he didn't even know. It would have been easy to look back and blame his ancestors for the reproach of Jerusalem, but Nehemiah looked within and blamed himself."[29] Not only does Nehemiah understand how the problem came to be, but he also knows that the solution starts with his confession.

In his love for Jerusalem, Nehemiah is concerned that he has done something to contribute to Jerusalem's current condition. Do we care and love those different from us enough to confess the sins of other people and sins that we may have committed that continue to perpetuate disunity? Love prompted Nehemiah to pray like this. When we engage others with the hope of unification, we should care enough for their plight to confess the sins that have been committed against them by others and repent of our acts of commission or omission towards them that have perpetuated the offense.

When we look at the divide in the church, our hearts should break like Nehemiah's. Afterward, like Nehemiah, we should go into prayer and take extreme ownership of what has caused the division. I understand that some people will say, "I didn't do anything wrong, or you can't blame me for this." If you read Nehemiah, we do not read about him making an excuse or telling God that he was in the palace serving the king, so Jerusalem's condition is not his problem. Nehemiah understood the gravity of the situation and took ownership of the sin that had created the problem.

Could it be that God desires us all to confess our sins that have led to the division before healing can occur? This type of confession is not about blaming one group for the existing division. Instead, it is about the people of God recognizing that the church walls are burning and that there continues to be division. It is about caring enough to lament over the current state of the church and asking God to forgive our forefathers and us for our sins. Only then will the actual change begin to occur.

Time To Change

By humbly presenting ourselves to God as a living sacrifice (Ro. 12:1-2), we can stay focused on pursuing unity and achieve this goal with renewed inspiration. Pastor and author H.B Charles once wrote, "There can be no spiritual unity unless there is true humility."[30] One aspect of humility is recognizing that we all have sinful residue on us after placing our faith in Jesus Christ as our Lord and Savior. For this residue to be continuously removed, believers in Christ must go through constant renewal. 2 Corinthians 4:16 says, "Though our outer self is wasting away, our inner self is being renewed day by day."

The idea of being renewed is to be changed into a new life from a corrupt state. It is a process where there is daily new growth in the life of a believer. This spiritual paradox of being corrupt and yet new is one that we must wrestle with and master. To master this spiritual paradox is to understand that even though we are positionally righteous in Christ (Romans 5:1), our day-to-day experiences do not always align with our heavenly position. God calls us to lay before Him daily to be more aligned with Him.

The act of going before the Lord will not happen accidentally. It must be a willful act of disconnection from the world and our selfish desires. It also means that we must give more deliberate attention to scripture. Giving priority to scripture leads us to the heart of God, and when we take the time to present ourselves to God and walk before Him, we allow Him to wash away the worldly nature and mindset in us. Being in His presence also heals the hurts and pains that we have experienced.

It also frees us from a lifestyle and philosophy that continues to fuel division. As believers, we cannot let the world's pollution influence us. God calls us to love one another unconditionally because His love is unconditional. Being in His presence allows us to love and extend grace to our brothers and sisters freely, even if we do not see eye-to-eye on a particular subject. And because we often disagree with others, going before the Lord must be a constant practice.

One Sunday, I recall holding the door open as people entered the church for worship. One of the white members said, "I normally tip my doorman." When he said that, it triggered some racist memories. At that moment, I was speechless. I thought to myself, "Is he joking? Did he just call me a doorman? Does he know who I am? Really dude."

I wanted to respond, but I knew my response would not be pleasant. If he could have read my mind, he would have been shocked at what I said to him. At this moment, I realized that the past anger and hurt from racism that I thought was gone wasn't. I needed to return to the

Father and lay my pain at His feet. I needed a renewal because those comments touched a nerve, so I put Romans 12:1-2 into practice:

> I appeal to you therefore, brothers, by the mercies of God, to present your bodies as a living sacrifice, holy and acceptable to God, which is your spiritual worship. Do not be conformed to this world, but be transformed by the renewal of your mind, that by testing you may discern what is the will of God, what is good and acceptable and perfect.

Pastor R. Kent Hughes has some convicting words for us regarding Romans 12:1-2. He says:

> The greater our comprehension of what God has done for us, the greater our commitment should be. Practically applied, Christ's gift, meditated on, accepted, taken to heart, is a magnet drawing us to deepest commitment to him. Immense vision will bring immense commitment...Paul does not ask for a favor when he says, "I appeal to you therefore, brothers, by the mercies of God..." but rather is stating an obligation. It is our obligation to think about what Christ has done and to make our commitment accordingly. There is scarcely anything more important for building our commitment than an increasing understanding of the greatness of God and his mercies to us...the totality of the commitment comes dramatically to us through the language of sacrifice.[31]

As I presented my anger and frustration to the Lord, I had to determine if I was mad because I thought the comment was a form of microaggression or because I felt that being a doorman was beneath me. Had I given up my rights to be acknowledged for my degrees and position? Am I committed enough to God to live up to my righteous responsibility to love my brother despite his comments? I thought, "Surely, as a pastor, he would not call me a doorman."

The Holy Spirit then challenged me. Do you think that being a doorman is beneath you? Can you not glorify the Father as a doorman? Can you still love that brother if you're a doorman? Being a living sacrifice and being renewed means being humbled and committed to the will of the Father and not my own. Having the capacity to serve and love those most that we think deserve it the least is how we keep our focus on God's glory. By doing this, we become more devoid of self and more complete in Him. By doing this, we become more devoid of self and more complete in Him.

In that moment at the church, I wanted to lash out, but in my quiet time later that week with the Lord, I realized that bringing the Father glory is not reacting with evil but with love. Even if the comment was racially motivated, my response must be motivated by the love of the Father. Dr. Martin Luther King Jr. once wrote, "Returning hate for hate multiplies hate, adding deeper darkness to a night already devoid of stars. Darkness cannot drive out darkness; only light can do that. Hate cannot drive out hate; only love can do that. Hate multiplies hate."[32] Like many others, I have come to understand that it takes more strength to love than to hate.

Any natural person can hate, which hardens our hearts toward the offender. It takes a person indwelled by the Holy Spirit to demonstrate love, kindness, and long-suffering to those who have hurt and offended us. Love is the only thing that can genuinely smother hate and be a catalyst for a heart change in others. Romans 12:1-2 reminds me of just how weak and broken I am and that I have to go before the Lord daily in the battle for unity in the church.

When we look at the depth and power of sin, we need to be convinced that to live a life that brings glory to the Father, we must always make it a priority to spend time with Him so that He can continue to conform us to the image of His Son even as we are being offended. When we do that, we can echo the words of Jesus on the cross. "Father forgive them for they know not what they do" (Luke 23:34). Disunity has plagued the church, and it needs to be eradicated. May we realize that we must be more concerned with glorifying the Lord to begin solving this problem.

As we focus on God's glory, He will reveal our shortcomings regarding unification. He will then call us to come into His presence and lay on His altar to perform brain surgery on us and cause our thinking to reflect more of His kingdom and not the world's. We must rise, embrace humility, allow God to heal our wounds, and walk in a manner worthy of the Lord. However, it will only happen when we focus on giving God glory in all we do. Ultimately, our unity displays God's glory and will help heal the divisions that have afflicted us for far too long.

6

Operating in God's Space

> *Behold, how good and pleasant it is when brothers dwell in unity!* — **Psalm 133:1**

Pastor and author Tim Keller once wrote,

> "In any relationship, there will be frightening spells in which your feelings of love dry up. And when that happens you must remember that the essence of marriage is that it is a covenant, a commitment, a promise of future love. So what do you do? You do the acts of love, despite your lack of feeling. You may not feel tender, sympathetic, and eager to please, but in your actions you must BE tender, understanding, forgiving and helpful. And, if you do that, as time goes on you will not only get through the dry spells, but they will become less frequent and deep, and you will become more constant in your feelings. This is what can happen if you decide to love."[33]

This should happen within the relationships of those in the body of Christ, not just those who are married. Becoming one as the people of God means that we must decide to love one another.

Love One Another

In eternity, love already exists between God the Father and Son. John 3:35 says, "The Father loves the Son and has given all things into his hand." In John 14:31, Jesus said, "...but I do as the Father has commanded me, so that the world may know that I love the Father." Jesus wanted the world to see how much he loved the Father, and he did so through humble submission, which was the visible demonstration of his love for the Father. This is further reinforced in Philippians 2:5-8 where it says:

> ⁵ Have this mind among yourselves, which is yours in Christ Jesus, ⁶ who, though he was in the form of God, did not count equality with God a thing to be grasped, ⁷ but emptied himself, by taking the form of a servant, being born in the likeness of men. ⁸ And being found in human form, he humbled himself by becoming obedient to the point of death, even death on a cross.

Just as there is unconditional love and oneness between the Father and Son, there must be unconditional love and oneness amongst God's people. This love must be submissive and intentional. The love we need to have for each other reaches across cultural boundaries to divest every form of prejudice, oppression, and discrimination. The measure of love is loving one another just as Jesus has loved us. This love leans into the lives of others and chooses to love them.

It is a love that seeks the betterment of others. Professor and theologian David Allen once wrote:

> It has occurred to me that perhaps the Bible has so much to say about Christians loving other Christians because it is such a hard thing to do...Jesus did not say people will know that we are his followers by our doctrinal orthodoxy but by our love...People will know that we are faithful followers of Jesus, not so much by what we

> know, but by what we do and how we love...There is no place for racism in the church. There is no place for hatred of an individual...Hatred leads to spiritual blindness. No way can we walk in the light and hate someone else. Hatred so zaps purpose and direction in life that you can't know God's direction for your life. Hatred takes you out of God's will. You cannot be in God's will and hate your brother.[34]

Knowing this, we must also embrace the fact that if we refuse to love one another the way Jesus loves us, we are not in God's will, and perhaps we are at risk of living out 1 John 2:9-11, which says:

> [9] "Whoever says he is in the light and hates his brother is still in darkness. [10] Whoever loves his brother abides in the light, and in him there is no cause for stumbling. [11] But whoever hates his brother is in the darkness and walks in the darkness, and does not know where he is going, because the darkness has blinded his eyes."

If we are going to live in unity, we have to stop living and thinking in darkness. We need to begin having conversations that will lead us to experience the freedom and joy that comes from unity. We are at the point where talking about unity in the church should go hand in hand with conversations about the purpose of the church. Just tolerating people in the body of Christ is not enough. We must embrace everyone, which includes their history, culture, and struggles. We need to move more towards redemptive thinking because it enables us to have solid doctrine and a biblical ethic to go with it.

Mark DeYmaz once wrote that "we must recognize that diverse people have been called not only to worship God but to walk and work together as one in and through the local church"[35] He also stated, "An increasingly diverse, painfully polarized and cynical society is no longer finding credible the message of God's love for all people as preached from segregated pulpits and pews."[36] To move forward as a loving community and truly embrace one another we need to embrace the ideology of living in a third space with other believers.

Our Spaces

Why is it so hard to love other people? We may have a vertical relationship with God, but because of our unique childhood experiences and what we have learned growing up, having horizontal relationships with others and loving them the way God requires can be very difficult. Many of our experiences shape us and move forward with us as we get older. Our attitudes, behaviors, the way we see the world, and even the way we dress can all be a result of what we experience as children. What stems from this is that we create a space we live in.

The space consists of how we view and respond to the world, the truths we believe, our faith perspective, things we may not want others to know about us, and other nuances. In our space, we tend only to welcome those with similar experiences and spaces. If people have experienced any abuse or other acute issues growing up, like divorce, their space may not be very inclusive of others who can't relate to those experiences. I believe this is why we have support groups and why people feel comfortable in those spaces. When we believe people resonate with our experiences, it brings us a level of comfort with them.

Also, within these spaces are our values. These are core principles that we have learned and now live by. Values such as working hard, not being late, or sharing with others can be ingrained in us, so much so that they govern how we live. For example, if you are a person who shows up early for appointments and thinks being on time is being late, then it probably irritates you when people are late.

You try to be patient with late people, and sometimes you bite your tongue instead of telling them how you feel about their lateness, but deep inside, it annoys you to no end. I am one of those people. In my ministry experience as a pastor, I have learned that it is hard for people to love each other when they have grown up differently, live in different spaces, and have opposing values. And as Christians, our natural tendency is to stay in our space because it is comfortable for us.

Growing up, I was picked on at school, my parents got divorced, and I was exposed to drugs. As I got older, because of my childhood experiences, I did not like being around people who talked about or teased other people. I did not value marriage, and I had no problem using drugs and being around other people who used drugs. However, I was also raised on certain values: respect your elders, always dress for success, speak articulately, and always be on time. My experiences growing up and the values I learned represented my space and how I lived. So much so that as I got older, many of my choices, actions, and the people I hung out with were based on the space that I created.

All of us have our own particular spaces driven by experiences and learned values. Whether it concerns lifestyle, ethnicity, character, morality, or family, our spaces determine what we will or won't accept as we relate to others. Included in those spaces are ideologies, beliefs, and idiosyncrasies that we hold tightly. In our spaces, we have our moral standards and learned practices. Our space ultimately represents who we are, and we get offended when anyone threatens that space. When there is a violation of our space, fear, anger, or confusion tends to be our natural response because there is an assumption that people should have an understanding of our space.

Have you ever found yourself saying or thinking things like, "You should know how I feel," "You should know what I believe," "You should know I don't like..." or "You should know better." Phrases like these presuppose that everyone should think and act like us or at least know how we think and act. Francis Schaeffer, theologian and pastor, once said, "People have presuppositions... By 'presuppositions,' we mean the basic way that an individual looks at life- his worldview. The grid through which he sees the world. Presuppositions rest upon that which a person considers to be the truth of what exists. A person's presuppositions provide the basis for their values and therefore the basis for their decisions."[37]

Because of our presuppositions, we have contributed to a culture of division. We live in our space with our presuppositions and deceive ourselves into believing that our thinking, lifestyle, morality, and values are correct and the best way to navigate through life. This leads to championing disillusionment and condemning anyone who is different or opposes our space. The sin in us presupposes that everyone should think, act, and respond like us; if they don't, something is wrong with them. Sin can also create unconscious bias in our space that impacts how we view people. Within this bias, we can give preferential treatment to one person over another. It is this same bias that can lead us to mistreat people and rely completely on our assumptions about them.

In many instances, people live in spaces absent a relationship with God. And because of that, it is even easier to walk away or "unfriend" those who are not like us. We draw lines in the sand and dare not listen to someone else's perspective. Much of our discord stems from retreating and staying in our spaces. The longer we stay there, the longer we become content with thinking we are always right.

Because of this, when one person in one space interacts with another person in another space, there will inevitably be conflict. When there are two different people from two different spaces coming together, instead of learning from each other by leaning into understanding, they tend to fight or withdraw from each other because they would rather be right in their minds than listen and learn from the other person. As followers of Christ, if we are to truly live unified when two conflicting spaces interact with each other, there needs to be a third space that regulates how we interact with one another.

Third Space

When we look at the great community in Acts 2:42, it says, "And they devoted themselves to the apostles' teaching and the fellowship, to the breaking of bread and the prayers." In this verse, those who believe are continuously engaged in and attentive to the authority of God's Word, fellowship, compassion towards one another, and prayer. But who are the "they" in the passage? Within the context of Acts 2, you had people from different nations, with cultural and language barriers, coming together via the Holy Spirit. And just like at Pentecost, today, the power of the Holy Spirit still draws different people together. It is the gospel of Jesus Christ that brings two people from two different spaces together and ushers them into a third space.

The third space is a spiritual environment, where God is the authority, and He governs how people learn and grow alongside each other. The character of the third space is one of love, grace, mercy, patience, and understanding. Within the third space, God's love that is growing in us is displayed toward other believers as we participate in community together, care for one another, worship together, and even disagree with one another, all under the authority of God. When two people humbly come together in the third space, they desire to be more like Jesus, so they will begin to surrender more to God and renounce all of their values and ideologies that do not reflect the kingdom of God.

In the third space, true unity starts to occur as our desires, intentions, worldviews, and actions become increasingly Christ-centered. It is the space where we come together as an intercultural family to study God's word and learn what it means to be one and live righteously. And because we are family, there are no presuppositions made because we know we are all broken; we can be ourselves, be accepted, argue, and ask questions to help us be better Christ-followers and better love and understand one another. As we grow, judgment of one another becomes less and less, we willingly show grace to each other, and the intersecting of individual lives occurs.

In his book, "Winning the Race to Unity," Dr. Clarence Shuler wrote about a conversation he had with a Christian friend who expressed that he understood that racism was wrong but did not know why. Later, they opened the Bible and began examining passages that dealt with racism. Dr. Shuler could have easily dismissed his friend's inquiry, but instead, he brought him into the third space (my interpretation) so that there could be healing and understanding of racial issues.

Dr. Shuler observed that many Christians are unaware of how the Bible speaks to prejudice, race, and cultural issues. The third space does not happen automatically. Dr. Shuler understood this and intentionally walked with his friend through this process.

In the same way, we must forsake our stereotypes, prejudices, and hate and walk with others. Psalm 34:14 says, "Turn away from evil and do good; seek peace and pursue it." Within biblical unity, there is a peace that is fueled by intentional love that drives us to sacrifice for others. New Testament scholar John Piper understood this when he wrote:

> "To be sure, unifying love in the body of Christ includes a rugged commitment to do good for the family of God whether you feel like it or not (Galatians 6:10). But, as difficult as it is for diverse people, the experience of Christian unity is more than that. It includes affectionate love, not just sacrifice for those you don't like. It is a feeling of endearment. We are to have affection for those who are our family in Christ. "Love one another with brotherly affection" (Romans 12:10). "Having purified your souls by your obedience to the truth for a sincere brotherly love, love one another earnestly from a pure heart" (1 Peter 1:22). "All of you, have ... sympathy, brotherly love, a tender heart, and a humble mind" (1 Peter 3:8)."[38]

We all have our spaces that have been shaped by experiences and values. And yet, in Christ, God calls us to a higher calling. It is a calling that requires intentional acts of love and sacrifice. Entering into the third space is a covenant decision where we find the strength to love, listen, and forgive one another. In the next chapter, we will see that when we enter the third space, we will have the opportunity to show our faith not just in words but in action. This is the path to lasting unity.

7

Faith in Action: Three Little E's

> *So also faith by itself, if it does not have works, is dead.*
> — James 2:17

Third space will become more of a reality as we cross cultural boundaries and build relationships with people. Just ask Dary Davis, a black man who befriended a Ku Klux Klan member. He stated in an interview, "If you spend five minutes with your worst enemy, you will find you have something in common…If you spend 10 minutes, you'll find you even have more in common. And the more you find that you have in common and build upon those things, the less the things that you have in contrast will begin to matter, like skin color."[39] When we enter the third space and allow God's agenda to be primary, we will learn that others in the space are not that different from us.

Author C.S. Lewis once wrote, "Friendship is born at that moment when one person says to another, 'What! You too? I thought I was the only one." We need the third space because God wants all of His children to be in a relationship, encouraging one another, empathizing and sympathizing with one another, and pushing one another to be more Christ-centered. The Father does not want His children to be at odds with one another or oppress one another. As the body of Christ, we must continue to embody community and begin building authentic Christ-centered relationships where we live out three critical components: 1) practicing equality, 2) providing equity, and 3) personifying equanimity. These three components represent our faith in action and how we are to engage others in the third space.

Practicing Equality

> [20] "I do not ask for these only, but also for those who will believe in me through their word, [21] that they may all be one, just as you, Father, are in me, and I in you, that they also may be in us.
> John 17:20-21

In the triune Godhead, there is equality amid diversity. John 1:1 says, "In the beginning was the Word, and the Word was with God, and the Word was God." In verse 14 And the Word became flesh and dwelt among us." Colossians 1:15 says, "The Son is the image of the invisible God...." The Trinity is equal in power, though their functions are different. One is not better or more important than the other. Jesus was the only one in the Godhead that put on human flesh, so their appearances are different. He is the only one in the Godhead who physically suffered, so they have different experiences. In the same way, in Christ, though we all have different appearances, experiences, gifts, and abilities allowed and given to us by God, all of us are equal. None of us is more important than the other. This is what unity looks like:

> For just as the body is one and has many members, and all the members of the body, though many, are one body, so it is with Christ. For in one Spirit, we were all baptized into one body—Jews or Greeks, slaves or free—and all were made to drink of one Spirit. For the body does not consist of one member but of many. If the foot should say, "Because I am not a hand, I do not belong to the body," that would not make it any less a part of the body. And if the ear should say, "Because I am not an eye, I do not belong to the body," that would not make it any less a part of the body. If the

> whole body were an eye, where would be the sense of hearing? If the whole body were an ear, where would be the sense of smell? But as it is, God arranged the members in the body, each one of them, as he chose. If all were a single member, where would the body be? As it is, there are many parts, yet one body. The eye cannot say to the hand, "I have no need of you," nor again the head to the feet, "I have no need of you." On the contrary, the parts of the body that seem to be weaker are indispensable, and on those parts of the body that we think less honorable we bestow the greater honor, and our unpresentable parts are treated with greater modesty, which our more presentable parts do not require. But God has so composed the body, giving greater honor to the part that lacked it, that there may be no division in the body, but that the members may have the same care for one another. If one member suffers, all suffer together; if one member is honored, all rejoice together. 1 Corinthians 12:12-26

A.W. Tozer once wrote, "Back on the farm in Pennsylvania, we had an old apple tree. It was a gnarly, stark-looking tree. A casual glance at this tree might tempt someone to pass it up. Regardless of how terrible the tree looked, however, it produced some of the most delicious apples I have ever eaten. I endured the gnarly branches in order to enjoy the delicious fruit."[40] This story by Tozer is a reminder that we cannot judge the fruitfulness of people based on their outward appearance.

The transition from division to unity is seeing others as valued, indispensable, gifted members of the family of God regardless of their outward appearance and before they do acts of service. Seeing people in the image of God first means believing that their gifts and uniqueness are more important than things like their ethnicity, financial status, or struggles. Many in the world have lost hope when it comes to equality. But we must remain vigilant to extend equality to all people.

Theologian St. Augustine has been known, though unconfirmed, to have said the following, "Hope has two beautiful daughters; their names are Anger and Courage. Anger at the way things are, and Courage to see that they do not remain as they are." The more we act in love and equality towards one another in the church, the more it will be seen by the world. As we in the church demonstrate equality towards each other, the hope we have becomes a link to Jesus for unbelievers. We are leading them from bondage to freedom as they experience the power of the Gospel that will hopefully lead them to experience and embrace the Gospel.

There is another aspect of equality that many tend to overlook, but one we must all practice. 1 Corinthians 12:12-26 declares that there is a diversity of gifts in the body of Christ. However, we cannot overlook verse 26: "If one part (*person*) of the body suffers, then the entire body (*everyone*) equally suffers, and if one part (*person*) is honored in the body, then the entire body (*everyone*) rejoices." A crucial part of equality is embracing and willingly walking with people in the body of Christ. Spencer Perkins wrote, "For it is only when we feel a friend's pain by making "his" problem "our problem" that we will harness the necessary passion to act."[41]

Equality is not just about treating all people the same. It is also about sharing life with people different from us. When we dwell with people, their concerns become our concerns, and their victories become our victories. For example, if my brother or sister in the faith struggles with overcoming abuse from the past, I am called to lean into their lives, embrace them, and allow their struggles to become my struggles. I am called to walk with them, listen to what they have gone through, and share their pain. During this process, I am also to encourage them, pray with them, and go through their healing journey with them. In essence, we need to start hanging out with people beyond Sundays and learn what life is like for them. When we do this, we will share in their pain and their joys.

In the third space, we are all at the table, helping and listening to one another from a Christ-centered perspective. When we are not willing to share life with others, we have no genuine commitment to equality. If we think of everyone as equals and never share their concerns and dismiss their issues, they are not equals in our hearts. As my equal, I want you to be concerned about me just as I am concerned about you. I love you as I love myself. If I know we are equals in my heart, then my actions will demonstrate that I share your burdens.

Providing Equity

> [22] The glory that you have given me I have given to them, that they may be one even as we are one- John 17:22

The glory given to Jesus by the Father is the glory of humble service. It is the glory of serving the Father; it is the glory of being sent to serve, and it is the glory of the cross. It is the glory of self-sacrifice. It is the glory of sharing burdens. It is the glory of absorbing faults. The glory of forgiveness. The glory of speaking the truth in love and holding others accountable. It is the glory of servant leadership. The glory of giving grace! That is the glory that Jesus has given to us. Our Christianity was never meant to be just intellectual or emotional. It is meant to be active and life-giving. And one way we can be life-giving is through the sharing of resources.

Our righteousness is not our own; it is the righteousness of Christ that has been imputed or given to us. Because of Jesus' resurrection, we, too, get to experience the resurrection. He gave of himself so that we could glorify the Lord and be better. And when we humbly serve each other, we give of ourselves so that our brothers and sisters can be better. We offer our resources, time, talent, and treasure so that others can be all that God has called them to be. Another word for this is equity. This is what it means to be a servant, and this is the glory that God has given us. That is seen in the great community in Acts 2:44-45.

> [44] And all who believed were together and had all things in common. [45] And they were selling their possessions and belongings and distributing the proceeds to all, as any had need.

These verses indicate that early Christians were devoted to one another in a way that transcended material possessions. As it pertains to the church in Acts 2, theologian William Barclay wrote, "It was a sharing Church where these early Christians had an intense feeling of responsibility for each other."[42] Providing equity to others is creating an atmosphere of fairness and justice by giving resources to those in need so that they can thrive. It is an understanding that, as believers in Christ, we have a biblical responsibility to support one another.

> "But if anyone has the world's goods and sees his brother in need, yet closes his heart against him, how does God's love abide in him? Little children, let us not love in word or talk but in deed and in truth."
> 1 John 3:17-18

This verse is not a passage imploring just the rich to help the poor. Providing biblical equity is not a responsibility solely for the rich. It is for anyone who has adequate resources to help someone else. Therefore, this passage is urging any believer to provide basic life necessities to those who are in need. This was not a form of socialism or welfare. The people genuinely cared for one another and were selling their possessions and distributing them to all who had need. It was also a reciprocal act when needed. The main point is that there was mutual generosity from everyone. Author Thabiti Anyabwile, when writing about demonstrating generosity towards others, said:

> We see how generous God has been to us in Christ; then we look with similar kindness on our neighbors. We recognize those who have no coats and no food while we have multiple coats and full cupboards. Many of us spend minutes in our closets deciding which coat best matches our shoes. How many schoolchildren did we pass on our way who needed a winter coat? How many homes did we pass in need of groceries? The repentant Christian life opens our eyes to

these things. God has been generous to us, and we are compelled to care for others. In repentance, we recognize that our abundance is to be shared in blessing our neighbors.[43]

Some may question how others may use the resources once they are given. By looking at 1 John 3:17-18, we understand that seeing a brother in need is to observe and discern their need. We are not giving resources away without any wisdom or discernment. We are still called to be good stewards of our resources. God has given us resources and wants us to give from a generous heart and not out of guilt or compulsion. It is a Christ-centered compelling that should drive us to recognize that we are blessed to be a blessing to others, especially those in the faith community.

When the apostle John speaks of the heart, he is speaking of compassion. If we love God, we should not disregard those in need. Tim Keller states, "The Bible depicts the human world as a profoundly interrelated community. So the godly must live in such a way that the community is strengthened."[44] When part of the body is in need, other parts should provide support, or the whole body suffers. For the early church, there was a sacrifice in the fellowship. R. Kent Hughes wrote:

> "True fellowship costs! So many people never know the joys of Christian fellowship because they have never learned to give themselves away. They visit a church or small study group with an eye only for their own needs (hardly aware of others) and go away saying, "There is no fellowship there." The truth is, we will have fellowship only when we make it a practice to reach out to others and give something of ourselves."[45]

Now, let's take this idea of equity to another level. God also calls us to utilize our influence to help others in need. By using our influence, we help give others opportunities. What this boils down to is a sharing of power. As followers of Christ, we are called to share our influential ability to help others in need willingly. Barnabas does this with Paul in Acts 9:27 where it says, "But Barnabas took him and brought him to the apostles and declared to them how on the road he had seen the Lord, who spoke to him, and how at Damascus he had preached boldly in the name of Jesus." Barnabas uses his status to vouch for Paul's transformation.

But look at what happens later...Paul, in turn, does the same for Timothy, in Philippians 2:19-20 when he writes, "I hope in the Lord Jesus to send Timothy to you soon, so that I too may be cheered by news of you. For I have no one like him, who will be genuinely concerned for your welfare." In the Third Space, when Christians treat others equitably, we inevitably provide Biblical justice to others in an unjust world. We also help other followers of Jesus thrive in worldly systems so that they can be a godly influence in the world.

Personifying Equanimity

> [26] I made known to them your name, and I will continue to make it known, that the love with which you have loved me may be in them, and I in them." John 17:26

According to John 17:26, Jesus gave and continues to give divine love to his disciples, empowering them to love the lost, triumph over adversity, humbly serve others, and endure all things and people. John Piper once wrote, "Hate serious blunders not sincere brothers."[46] David Allen wrote:

> "One of the ways that we demonstrate spiritual maturity is by how we love one another as brothers and sisters in the faith. This demonstration of love towards others is achieved as the love of God is continuously poured into us. "Loving one another...is both a duty and a test. It is a duty in that we are commanded as Christians to practice love. It is a test in that our practice of love for others demon-

strates the reality of our Christian faith...It is not enough to believe rightly. We must behave rightly."[47]

I have been married for 17 years, and it took six months of marriage to realize my wife wasn't perfect. But it took me ten years to realize that those imperfections wouldn't change overnight. In the past seven years of my marriage, I have learned what it means to practice patience with my wife. If you ask her, I am sure she will say the same about me, although she has probably needed a lot more patience and time to deal with me.

Colossians 3:13 says, "bearing with one another and, if one has a complaint against another, forgiving each other; as the Lord has forgiven you, so you also must forgive." In this passage, the idea of "bearing" means to endure with evenness of temper continuously. Another word for this is equanimity. This may not be tough for you, but it is for me. When there is equanimity, there is mental calmness and the ability to sustain and endure when dealing with others because we recognize that none of us are perfect.

Dr. John Perkins once said to me, "Love binds and brings us together." This type of love only comes from the Father because He embodies love. Think about the love that God has for you. How patient has he been with you as you continue to live a mixed life with good and evil? Has God kept a record of your wrongs? As selfish as we are, even after acknowledging Jesus as our Lord and Savior, the Father continues to show His love, compassion, grace, and mercy toward us during the ups and downs of our walk with Him.

A.W. Tozer said it best, "Remember that it is only by the infinite patience of God that we are not consumed."[48] Psalm 103:8 says, "The Lord is merciful and gracious, slow to anger and abounding in steadfast love." Perfect patience is a part of the nature of God. If we abide in the third space, we must learn to bear with one another because we *all* fall short of God's glory. It seems as though we often place too high of an expectation on people. How naive it is for us to expect perfection from the imperfect. Francois Fenelon sums it up perfectly when he says, "You really don't understand how far man has fallen if you expect any good from him."[49]

We profess people are imperfect, yet we get mad when people do things that go against the will of God. Or when people make honest mistakes, we are easily offended and ready to give them a piece of our minds because we are the "Christian police." Living out the truth that none of us is perfect should provide us with the proper perspective of humanity. All of us are prone to think and do unrighteous things, say something that offends others, make poor decisions, or have an emotionally off day. Knowing this, as the body of Christ, it is our responsibility to personify equanimity with one another. Embedded within this patience is understanding offenses. Bishop Noel Jones once said:

> Now it's impossible to live without being offended. There's nobody absolutely no one, who has not been offended by somebody and nobody in this place has not hurt somebody themselves. So if there are two things that I can declare to be right today, it is that you have offended and hurt somebody in your life and somebody has hurt you. [50]

In life, it is indeed impossible not to offend or be offended. But as followers of Jesus, we must still live out Ephesians 4:32, "Be kind to one another, tenderhearted, forgiving one another, as God in Christ forgave you."

We are in covenant together, united by the blood of Jesus, and we must love each other and bear with one another. Taking hold of the cross will call us, at times, to silently endure the folly and ignorance of others and extend mercy. We must violently resist the temptation to withhold grace and mercy from others when they say or do something that offends us. As you read this, you may be thinking of people you don't like and find it hard to bear their issues. I understand. Even as I write this, I can also think of some people whose struggles I find hard to bear. Yet, to bear with one another falls under the umbrella of loving them. Martyn Lloyd-Jones took it to another level when he wrote:

> Liking is a matter of personal preference. Loving is a matter of obedience to Christ and the Word of God. Love penetrates beyond the superficial and moves to the essence of the person. It overcomes obstacles and excuses. Love sees beyond what it does not like in a person and minimizes it in order to see the person as Christ sees him. Then seeing the person in that way opens the door to acting toward that person in a Christlike way. Loving people you don't like means treating them as if you did like them! You choose to act toward them in a way that is pleasing to Christ and that exhibits how Christ would act toward them. The nature of Christian love is that it acts, it gives, it expresses itself towards others.[51]

Today, too many of our churches are filled with Christians who are unwilling to bear with others, but we would never admit that. We just walk around with a veneer of Jesus and fake it until we get home so we can speak negatively about the people we worshiped with. As we continuously turn our will to God's will and express that intention through word and deed, we need to begin to invite others into the space of patience and love. As followers of Christ, we are called to endure the faults of others because we recognize that we, too, fall short, we offend, we want others to be patient with us, and we want to be loved by others the way God loves us. With patience and compassion, we can love like this and bear with one another, but it is an intentional act of the will to see God work in and through us for His glory.

Unity is not automatic. It requires followers of Jesus to journey with people different than them willfully. In the third space, where cultural boundaries are transcended, we will cultivate powerful relationships. Not only are these relationships grounded in equality, equity, and equanimity, but they also demonstrate God's transformative work in all of us. This, my friend, becomes a catalyst for change in the church that has been marred by division.

8

Loving People God's Way

> *Beloved, let us love one another, for love is from God, and whoever loves has been born of God and knows God.*
> — 1 John 4:7

In 2019, I had the opportunity to go to Atlanta, GA, to visit the National Center for Human and Civil Rights. When we arrived, I had no idea what to expect. My pastor and I went together to prepare for a multiethnic doctoral course we would co-teach later that year. Part of the class required the students to go to the center as a group, so we decided to go early to get a lay of the land and ensure that we were not caught off guard by anything. Once we entered the center, we were immediately thrust into the civil rights movement.

Interactive displays with video recordings showed how racist the South had become. Then I looked to my left and saw different states and the different Jim Crow laws for each state. I had thought that the laws were the same no matter where you were in the South, but that was not the case. I was amazed at how sinister and ridiculous some of the laws were. For example, in Georgia, it was unlawful for an amateur white baseball team to play baseball on any lot, even a vacant one, that was within two blocks of black residents.

In Louisiana, it was a misdemeanor for a landlord to rent any part of the building to black tenants if the building was already partly occupied by white tenants. It was a misdemeanor to have anything written, printed, or typewritten that promoted social equality in Mississippi. With so many different laws in each state, black people who abided by Jim Crow laws in Mississippi could be lawbreakers once they went to Louisiana because of their different Jim Crow laws. As I was reading all of this, I could feel the anger bubbling within me.

That anger towards white people that I thought was gone started to rise. Maybe it was righteous indignation, but I highly doubt it. Just as we were about to step away from the Jim Crow laws exhibit, one of the employees, an African-American man, approached us and asked, "Do you know why Jim Crow was established?" He then looked at me and asked the question again. He added, "As a black man, you should know this." Ouch! Talk about calling a brother out. I thought about his question and said, "Because of hate." He responded, "No. The reason why Jim Crow was instituted was to prevent the two communities from ever coming together."

He then repeated, "The reason Jim Crow was instituted was to prevent the two communities from ever coming together." That's all he said. I was expecting something profound. But that was it. However, I thought about what he said as we walked away. I then saw pictures of the Freedom Riders. Within this beautiful collage of pictures were black and white people who walked alongside one another and rode the bus together for civil rights. I kept thinking, "Why haven't the communities come together? There is so much beauty when we embrace different ethnicities. Why are churches still intentionally segregated?"

As I processed this, the word that kept coming to mind was "fear." Fear is the enemy of love. White people feared what they did not know and thought black people were inferior. They wanted to prevent the white and black communities from coming together out of fear. Fear made them believe that it would hurt their own culture. Their fear drove them to take the easy way out. Fear was driving their space. The fear manifested itself into hate, which led them to think anyone who was not white was also not educated or civilized.

I thought it was flat-out hatred, but fear was at the root of hate. Fear created the separation because, back then, many white people thought this was the best solution for everyone. Instead of learning to love and deepen relationships with black people, they did the opposite. They further learned to hate out of their fear and further separated.

Then I thought about people at the other end of the spectrum. I thought about anyone whose skin was olive-toned or darker dealing with the hurt of being highly mistreated and the fear of being killed. That hurt ran so deep, and that fear was so entrenched in many hearts that non-whites did not see unity with white people as remotely possible. William Shakespeare once wrote in *The Tempest*, "What's past is prologue" or simply put, history determines the future. If we hold to that statement, the fear that catalyzed the hate that created Jim Crow laws and the hurt and oppression inflicted on anyone not white, which led to fear of death, continues to stimulate division today.

Even with the transformative power of the gospel, this fear still permeates within the church because people have brought their spaces into it and have not surrendered them to God, which is why the church continues to be segregated ethnically and culturally. We cannot deny that our current cultural climate is still under the oppressive ideology of slavery and Jim Crow. Whether it is xenophobia, homophobia, androphobia (fear of men), agoraphobia (fear of sexual abuse), or any phobia related to dealing with other people, we continue to allow fear to drive us and act in ways that are contrary to scripture. Again, the fears that we have are legitimate. So, let's examine fear briefly by going back to the Garden of Eden.

Love Over Fear

In Genesis 1:26, God said, "Let us make man in our image, after our likeness." Once Adam was created, God provided him with a helper, Eve. The two were able to dwell in community with one another, and they were naked, unashamed, and respected each other. Within this honorable community, God told Adam in Genesis 1:28, "Be fruitful and multiply and fill the earth and subdue it, and have dominion over the fish of the sea and over the birds of the heavens and over every living thing that moves on the earth." God was calling Adam and Eve to reproduce and continue building a noble and virtuous community that reflected the glory of God, the image and likeness of God, and to be His people who demonstrated honor and respect for God, one another, and creation.

In Genesis 2, God specifically commanded Adam not to eat from the tree of the knowledge of good and evil. However, in chapter 3, Eve took it upon herself to eat the fruit after being deceived by the serpent and thinking that it would be suitable for her. In her folly, she decided to determine what was good, which was something only God had decided until this point. In her futile attempt to be like God after eating the fruit, the Bible says in Genesis 3:6 that she gave some to Adam.

By eating the fruit, Adam participated in what he thought was good, but it was evil. In Genesis 3:8-10, we read, *"And they heard the sound of the LORD God walking in the garden in the cool of the day, and the man and his wife hid themselves from the presence of the LORD God among the trees of the garden. But the LORD God called to the man and said to him, "Where are you?" And he said, "I heard the sound of you in the garden, and I was afraid, because I was naked, and I hid myself."* The Hebrew word for afraid is translated as "yare," which means "absolutely in fear." After his sin, Adam is in complete fear because he knows that the consequence of his action is death (Genesis 2:17). As a result of this fear, Adam decides to hide.

According to Genesis 1 and 2, Adam and God had a perfect relationship until this moment. God provided all that Adam needed. He gave Adam responsibility, dominion, and companionship. And even though God did all of that and demonstrated His holy character to Adam, Adam's first response to his sin was to hide because he was afraid. Another way to articulate Adam's response to God is, "I heard you in the garden, and I *separated* myself from you." In addition to his sin spiritually separating him from God, Adam invokes physical segregation between him and God. Why? Because he was afraid.

We are not told in the biblical text that Adam knew about the attributes of God. Did he know that God was compassionate, gracious, and merciful? He knew that he would die from eating from the tree of the knowledge of good and evil, but that is all he knew. Even with his seemingly limited understanding of God, the one thing Adam knew how to do naturally after demonstrating fear was to segregate himself from God. Out of fear, Adam hides, and as a result of Adam's sin of eating the fruit, the fear he experiences causes him to further sin by putting the blame squarely on God and Eve (Genesis 3:12).

Talk about self-preservation. But why did Adam eat the fruit? Perhaps, like Eve, he too got caught up in thinking that he also knew what was good, which led to sin, fear, and separation. What we do see is that fear, as a result of sin, like Adam, will cause us to separate from others, leaving us isolated. For example, for some people, if we think we have offended someone, we will not talk to them or avoid them altogether out of fear. In his fear, Adam blamed God and Eve. First eating the fruit and now finger-pointing. Talk about an epic fail.

This spiritual negligence where sin is compounded not only got Adam, but it still gets us today. As a result of Adam's sin, God's love interceded. Genesis 3:21 says, "And the LORD God made for Adam and for his wife garments of skins and clothed them." The Lord took extreme measures to restore the relationship with His creation. But this is what love does. It seeks to rescue and redeem even that which is entirely depraved, guilty, and fearful. Love fights to overcome fear.

As followers of Christ, we must love others like this. The hope revealed in God's word is that He relentlessly pursues a relationship with us even when we reject Him. He still seeks community with us. There is no fear in God because He is perfect love. In like manner, because He has given us His Spirit, we also do not need to live in fear of embracing others. Fear of others who were different was the catalyst that created Jim Crow laws, and it is that same fear that continues to create division in the church. As uncomfortable as it is, we must depend on God and not let fear hold us hostage in our pursuit of unity and stop us from loving people.

We live in a world where we have the opportunity to demonstrate love to all people each day. Love cannot just be verbally expressed. It requires action and can no longer be a secondary issue. More importantly, loving others cannot be a choice. God does not choose to love us. He loves us because He is love. 1 John 4:7-8 says, "Beloved, let us love one another, for love is from God, and whoever loves has been born of God and knows God. Anyone who does not love does not know God because God is love." Everything that God does is in love because love is His character. The same must be true for Christians.

Love is a fruit of the Holy Spirit, so our character must be one of love. And if love is the foundation of our nature, we will demonstrate a relentless love for others regardless of our differences. People know we are followers of Christ not from the proclamation of love but from the actions of love. That is what sets us apart from the world. We should be known by the quality of our actions and not the quantity of our words.

God demonstrated his love for Adam and Eve by action. He redeemed them, and He showed love for us by His act of giving us Jesus. Therefore, we are called to demonstrate love by the activity of loving others. A mustard seed of love can tear down a mountain of fear. We must band together and let the world see how the love of God demonstrated through His children brings people together and gives people hope by keeping us together.

Love Battles To Affirm Dignity

John Perkins once wrote:

> The oppressor and the oppressed reflect a damaged image of God and long to express their creativity and dignity in a healthy way. For very different reasons, both the oppressed and the oppressor can be hard to love. But Jesus calls us as His followers to love our enemies

and also to care for the downtrodden, whether they are in a concentration camp in Germany or in a halfway house in Jackson, Mississippi. Dignity is worth the fight.[52]

One of the greatest battles in the fight for unity is the battle to affirm the dignity of other people. Let's look again at Genesis. God initially gave Adam and Eve dignity as He created humanity because they were made in His image and likeness. Dignity was inherent in humanity.

After the fall, Adam no longer glorifies God, and Adam is now dishonoring God. Not only that, but Adam has also dishonored his wife. He says, "The woman whom you gave to be with me, she gave me fruit of the tree, and I ate" (Genesis 3:12). So Adam has sinned by eating the fruit, and he compounds the issue by not taking ownership of his sin. He criticized God and blamed his wife, who he now calls just "the woman." To give someone dignity is to honor and respect them.

In one chapter, Adam has gone from affirming his wife's dignity (bone of my bone and flesh of my flesh) to dishonoring her (the woman you gave me). As a result of sin and fear, Adam disrespected God and his wife. Eve's dignity has been broken by the one who is supposed to esteem her. Adam's sin led to dishonor and disrespect for his wife, and it was the love of God alone that restored the lost dignity.

Like Adam and Eve, God came and rescued us by sending His only Son. In this godly walk, we are being regenerated and renewed by the Holy Spirit so that our physical practice of faith lines up with our spiritual position of being declared righteous. But in our pursuit of holiness, some of our selfishness is still present, so we must be vigilant and intentional to lay our hearts before God daily and use kingdom language (which we will discuss later) as we interact with others. As sons and daughters who are sealed with the Holy Spirit, we positionally bear the full image of Christ. And because of that position, our dignity is affirmed in 1 Peter 2:9, " But you are a chosen race, a royal priesthood, a holy nation, a people for his own possession, that you may proclaim the excellencies of him who called you out of darkness into his marvelous light."

From this affirmation of salvation (chosen people), dignity (royal priesthood), and new identity (holy nation), we should see the same attributes in those who are different from us in the body of Christ. They, too, have been redeemed and bear the same image. No matter if someone is young or old, healthy or sick, Republican or Democrat, male or female, the success of oneness is seen when we live as one in a godly community and treat one another with respect and honor. If we limit our love to only those who look, think, and act like us, we have shifted away from the heart of God, stripped others of their dignity, and further perpetuated the enemy's plan to divide.

Today, the critical problem in the body of Christ is that instead of affirming the God-given dignity that we all possess, many tend to perpetuate the schemes of the enemy by disparaging others because they are different. As God's creation and those who have been redeemed, we should value one another and affirm one another regardless of differences. To not do so tarnishes God's reputation. Affirming dignity in others starts with the complete surrender of self to God.

As we surrender more to Him, we realize that He is greater than we ever thought, and we are worse than we can imagine. But surrendering is not easy, given where we come from. Titus 3:3 says, "For we ourselves were once foolish, disobedient, led astray, slaves to various passions and pleasures, passing our days in malice and envy, hated by others and hating one another." Before Jesus, the flesh had ruled all of us, were disobedient, and related wrongly to others. Thomas Manton, a Puritan clergyman, once wrote,

> ...the self which we must hate or deny is that self which stands in opposition to God, or in competition with Him, and so jostles with Him for the throne. Lay aside God and self steps in as the next heir; it is the great idol of the world ever since the Fall. When men were so bold as to depose and lay aside God, self succeeded to the throne.[53]

We try to be our own gods and live life our way as completely selfish beings. Doing so has led to us experiencing our fair share of broken relationships. Our selfishness allows us to hurt others easily. This type of life does not simply disappear after we surrender to Jesus. Defaulting to hate or mistreating others may become a temptation for some, but praise God that there is good news after Titus 3 verse 3:

> [4] But when the goodness and loving kindness of God our Savior appeared, [5] he saved us, not because of works done by us in righteousness, but according to his own mercy, by the washing of regeneration and renewal of the Holy Spirit, [6] whom he poured out on us richly through Jesus Christ our Savior, [7] so that being justified by his grace we might become heirs according to the hope of eternal life.

Those of us who were once alienated from God have been given the right to be heirs and co-heirs with Christ. This new nobility, via salvation, takes us back to the way God created us. It takes us back to the dignity we were created to have before the fall. Therefore, dignity is an inherited trait of being an image-bearer of God and should thus be affirmed within the body of Christ.

In Luke 7, Jesus encounters a woman at the home of a Pharisee. The woman in the story is considered by most to be a "loose woman." Yet, with unflinching confidence, this woman came into the home, took out some perfume, and then anointed and kissed the feet of Jesus. During this time, Jesus could have quickly rejected her, made a joke about her profession, or said something sarcastic about her.

However, Jesus, as He always does, responds to the woman in the opposite manner that many men in his day would have. He was compassionate and forgiving. He affirmed her efforts and what she did by saying, "Your sins are forgiven" (Luke 7:48). Though it is not recorded in the text, I would believe that the woman's dignity and self-respect skyrocketed that day. She is now a daughter of the KING!

PEOPLE SUCK, GOD IS GOOD

Between 1999 and 2006, I worked in corporate America. In most of the meetings, my colleagues were predominantly white. During these meetings, I would be subjected to people greeting me by saying, "Yo, Yo, Yo...wassup?" Some would even ask me if I was bringing fried chicken to the staff potluck luncheon. Comments like these, unknown to them, always made me feel like an outsider and that I did not bring value to the organization. At times, I felt like the token black guy.

There were other days when I had shut down and did not interact with people because I feared that they would crack a "black joke" or make a stereotypical remark with the expectation that I would laugh and agree with it. I just chalked it up to people suck. This is not me pointing fingers because I also must admit that I have been in all-black spaces and have made many whites, Asians, and Latinos in the group feel uneasy. After all, hurt people will hurt people, and oppressed people will oppress people.

When anyone is a part of the dominant culture in a specific setting that is more suitable to the dominant group, it is easy to make those we think are different feel unwanted. We can unconsciously make people feel that they are not valued. We make disparaging and disrespectful statements about how people were raised, their accents, their food, and their dress. All of this is done with little to no thought about how our comments impact people. Unethical behavior and comments like this are not reflective of God's heart.

The problem is that we often limit the extension of our love to others because of differences. We refuse to lean into other cultures and experiences because we fear what is foreign to us. But the command of Jesus is clear, "Love your neighbor." Love here is not just about actions towards others; it is also about how we esteem others in our hearts. There is no qualifier (black, white, Asian, Latino, nice, mean, affluent, healthy, sick, poor, differently abled) specifying who my neighbor is.

The moment we act in ways that contradict God's second great commandment, we begin to tear down our neighbors. And as we knowingly or unknowingly tear them down, we begin to devalue and dishonor them, which takes away their dignity. Once that person's dignity is broken, that person can slowly drift into discouragement. This discouragement then leads to bondage of the heart and mind. This is why some people are fearful of speaking up, being judged, or potentially being treated as inferior.

At some point, they stopped being esteemed, and their dignity was impacted. And in their minds, it makes no sense to speak up if it only leads to mistreatment or being the butt of a joke. So, not speaking up becomes a form of self-protection. If not addressed, they can begin to think and act like they are inferior. This mindset flies in the face of God's original design for them and contradicts how they should think about themselves after they have been redeemed. Not affirming the dignity of our brothers and sisters in Christ can be the impetus that leads them to act out and live in a manner that is not Christ-centered.

Love Battles to Not Label

Phaedrus, a Roman fable writer and poet, once said, "Things are not always what they seem; the first appearance deceives many." There are several things that, when you look at them, appear to be one thing, but they are, in fact, something else entirely. A lead pencil does not contain lead but graphite. A firefly is not a fly but a beetle. Shortbread is not bread; it's a cookie. A cucumber is not a vegetable; it's a fruit.

I have a habit of taking people out to lunch who want to talk with me or hang out. One day, I met with a brother for lunch, and we started talking about politics and economics. As he was speaking, he said, "Malcolm, I know you are probably a Democrat." My initial thought was, "Wow, what would make you think that?" I then shared with him some positive reviews about Thomas Sowell, an American economist, and that I do not watch CNN or Fox News. I could tell by the look on his face that he was somewhat perplexed.

He tried to put me into his stereotypical box, but I would not fit. I went on to ask him about his life and his family. I wanted him to know that I care about him as a person and not his political affiliation.

The more we talked, the more we realized that we had some things in common. We shared some of our life goals with each other, and by the end of lunch, we were encouraging one another as brothers in Christ. The following Sunday, his wife came to me and said, " I don't know what happened or what you said at lunch, but it impacted my husband's perspective.

I have learned that we can be quick to label people and project onto them a false narrative that we have created because of our narrow framework of life. If we would take the time and listen to people, we can avoid jumping to rash opinions about them. The problem is that often; we can be so disturbed by the behavior and beliefs of others that our basic instinct as fallen beings is to judge them quickly. We look at the outward appearance or actions and never contemplate the heart behind the action. By listening to others and avoiding rash judgment, we have more of an opportunity not to let our feelings guide us when engaging others. C.S. Lewis wrote, "What you see and what you hear depends a great deal on where you are standing. It also depends on what sort of person you are."[54]

Many, many, many years ago, Jesus encountered a woman who was at a well all by herself. As the story goes, in John 4, Jesus has an entire conversation with her even though she has probably been labeled by many as a moral outcast. During this encounter, Jesus demonstrates sympathy towards her and breaks down social barriers by speaking with her. He respects her and does not label her according to her sins. He gives her a second chance at life. He was interested in her life and what she had to say. Her eternity and not her past or present condition was his concern.

One of my fears as a black man being in predominantly white spaces is being labeled "the angry black guy." I have been in several meetings, corporate and church, where someone says something that I am vehemently against. I will often challenge their position with tact and well-thought-out speech. If they come across as if they don't want to accept what I am saying, which I know is true, I have to control myself because even though I want to be more aggressive in my approach, I don't want them to label me as "The Angry Black Guy." In my opinion, not too many black men like to be labeled that guy, but more importantly, no one likes to be labeled.

After one staff meeting, one of my white coworkers asked me a question but prefaced it with, "I am not a racist or anything like that; I just want to ask you a question." This has happened to me several times, and I understand that there is a legitimate fear among some white people that they will be labeled as racist for asking a question. Some never even ask a question because of that fear. I truly believe that being labeled a racist is sometimes forced on white folks from other white folks who suffer from their own white guilt. I also believe that it is easy for anyone not white to quickly label white people as racist, given the issues we deal with in our country.

When either of these happens, over time, the person who received the label will eventually shut down and never want to have another conversation about racism or issues about ethnicity because they have been told that they are racist. The fear of being labeled as a racist does not motivate anyone to pursue unity. It is hard to live in an authentic community if I am constantly concerned about someone labeling me.

As Christians, we have all heard stories of people not wanting to go back to our churches because they thought people were labeling them the first time they went. We are quick to defend our church. But the truth is that it probably did happen because labeling people is what we naturally do, and it takes minimal effort to do it. It takes intentionality and effort to get to know people, but it can be challenging.

Let me be even more vulnerable – as a black man, if I am made to feel inferior in a predominantly white space, the chances of me telling that to my white counterparts is slim to none, especially if I believe that they actually look at me that way. To go and tell them how I feel, in my mind, may give them the ammunition to say, "We got him." So, instead of talking with them, I go to my safe black circle of friends and express my true feelings. They will encourage me, and some will tell me to quit, but at least I can express how I feel without being labeled. I then go back to work with a chip on my shoulder, a little bit of an attitude, and maybe a harder work ethic, and my white counterparts have no idea of the battle that is going on within me. Do I walk in the Spirit and love them or walk in the flesh and be the angry black guy?

On the flip side, I have spoken to several of my white friends and counterparts about their fear of being labeled. During a conversation with a dear brother of mine, he told me that he had some of his white friends at his house, and they were talking about the current issues in America. He overheard them say things that they probably would not say around black people. He also told me that they did not say anything inherently wrong. He just knew if they said it around black people, they would probably be labeled racist. There are things that white people say when they are only around white people because they fear that others may think that they are judgmental, discriminatory, or racist. Once again, the fear of being labeled is not just a black thing; it is an all-of-us thing.

Let's take it one step further. Many of us find ourselves in spaces, even Christian spaces, where we are not comfortable talking, and we hide our true feelings out of fear of being labeled. We are at a point in society, even in the church, where presenting one's ideologies will get you labeled as intolerant, racist, or sexist. Environments seem to be no longer conducive to being honest in speaking with one another. And yet, the Bible tells us in Ephesians 4:25, "Therefore, having put away falsehood, let each one of you speak the truth with his neighbor, for we are members one of another."

Another complementary verse is Colossians 3:9-10, "Do not lie to one another, seeing that you have put off the old self with its practices and have put on the new self, which is being renewed in knowledge after the image of its creator." We live in a culture where hiding our true feelings and labeling one another is common. As members of the body of Christ, we should be able to freely express ourselves tactfully without worrying if we will get labeled. We should also stop using labels that prevent community.

In the Fall of 2020, I visited a white student at Columbia International University. As we sat and talked, an African-American pastor and professor asked me to meet with him later, but I was unsure how to get to his office. The student decided to walk with me and show me where to go, and as we were walking, he said that he had been invited to a church but decided not to go because it was a black church, and he may not fit in. I told him that he should have gone for the experience. He admitted that he probably missed out on a great experience, and because of his fear of not fitting in or being seen a certain way, he probably missed out on a divine experience and encounter with God.

I resonate with that because there are times when I do not go into predominantly white spaces because I feel like I don't fit in, and they may see me a certain way. From the interaction with the student, I am further convinced that the fear of being labeled and labeling others drives people to withdraw from community and robs people of opportunities and diverse experiences where they can encounter God. Therefore, we must love without labeling. 1 John 4:18 says, "There is no fear in love, but perfect love casts out fear...." If we are one in Christ, we should be walking in love and creating environments of love where people feel safe about sharing their struggles, hurts, frustrations, and questions. Our aim should be to support one another to do good works, lift each other up, and not spew out words that wrongly define people based on the narrative we have given them.

Love Battles for Unity

In 2016, I was not serving in the church, nor did I have a desire to serve. I had gone through church hurt and did not take the time to heal from it. As a result, my marriage started going through a rough patch. I remember asking my wife if she wanted to leave me because I wanted to leave me. I loved her, but I hated myself. And because of my self-hatred, I did not think she needed to put up with me.

I shared with her all of my mess, struggles, and hurts because she needed to know, and I wanted to honor God. As I confessed my sins and emotions to her, I also shared that I was not the husband or father she needed me to be. I was perfectly content to let her walk away and live her life without me. At that moment, in my mind, she was better off not having to deal with me. After I shared my heart with her, and as we both were crying, she put her arms around me and lovingly said, "I forgive you." This was a pivotal point in our marriage and my life.

In the past, I had preached about the unconditional love of God, His grace that reaches the uttermost to save, and His forgiveness that can overcome any sin. Still, at this point, I was truly experiencing the love, grace, and forgiveness I had preached about. It was no longer theory or just words I read in the Bible. My wife embodied love and forgiveness so that we could remain unified.

From that point on, we made it a point to fight for our marriage each day. And each day, we battle our flesh and die to self so that we can truly love one another. We battle against our expectations of each other. We battle against criticizing each other. We battle against being sarcastic towards one another. It is a constant battle to love in order to remain as one.

In light of the Gospel, we cannot fall to the temptation to hate as the world hates, divide as the world divides, and cancel as the world cancels. There must be a deeper commitment not to repay division with division because that is what Satan wants. Jesus did not die for us so that we would remain divided. And as followers of Christ, we must battle to love others.

I was invited to a prayer video conference call with mostly white people who wanted to pray for black pastors. I was told just to call in, state my name, and be quiet. I did as I was told, and during the prayer, one of the white men confessed his past sins, what he was doing to hinder the advancement of black Americans, and that he wanted to change. After he prayed, a white woman confessed that she had intentionally looked over black women for jobs because they were black.

Another prayed about how they disregarded other people's struggles because they had not experienced their issues.

Hearing this melted my heart because when they first started praying, I thought, "Here are more prayers by white people who do not want to change. These prayers will be so generic." But to my surprise, the prayers were personal. They were prayers of love battling against the sins of racism and prejudice. And hearing them softened my heart. This was the beginning of change for them, and I also changed. This is what it looks like to battle for unity.

When I was in my early twenties, I had an x-ray taken of my teeth. The x-ray revealed that all of my wisdom teeth were impacted and needed to be surgically removed. The surgeon told me that I would be in great pain after the procedure but that even with all the pain, it was better to get it done. I agreed to the surgery, and after waking up from the procedure, I was in great pain. The surgeon told me that during the surgery, my teeth were more impacted than he thought. So, he had to pull harder to get the teeth out. He said it took longer than he thought, but that was the reason I was in so much pain after the procedure.

The same is true when fighting for unity. A collective x-ray of our hearts has been taken, and we have been impacted by sin, so much so that we will have to love each other harder to repair the damage that division has created. One of the most potent weapons we have for creating unity is love. It is a love that moves beyond labels and recognizes the dignity every person carries as an image-bearer of God.

Just as my wife demonstrated love for me, our love for others has the power to heal wounds and unify. The battle may be just as painful as removing impacted wisdom teeth, but it is a fight worth fighting. Yes, there will be some discomfort, and we may have to work harder. But in the end, it is worth the fight.

9

Eyes of Grace

> *...For the Lord sees not as man sees: man looks on the outward appearance, but the Lord looks on the heart.*
> — **1 Samuel 16:7**

My father was a charismatic man. At any given function, he was the center of attention. He could talk with anyone and make them feel like the most important person in the world. My father was also a jokester. He liked laughing and having a good time. There would be times when we would go to the store, and he would make up songs using the grocery list that my mom had given him.

However, he had his own issues. He was a rolling stone. Even though he had a family, he just couldn't settle down. He was also into drugs. Since I was a child, I can only tell you what was told to me. He was into marijuana and cocaine. Overall, my father lived a fast lifestyle, and this eventually led to my parents getting a divorce. After the divorce, my relationship with my dad went downhill.

He started dating another lady and became a father to her children, which meant my sister and I were an afterthought. My father then became "that dad." He was that dad who broke his promises and never came to milestone moments in my life. He did not come to my high school graduation, college graduation, seminary graduation, or my wedding. He became the dad who hardly kept his word, and after he broke a promise, he would try to talk his way back into my good graces.

In 2004, after I started going to seminary, I decided to forgive my father. I did not want his behavior to continue to have power over me. I called him, and after we moved beyond the pleasantries of the conversation, here is what happened:

Me: Hey, I just called to tell you that I forgive you.
Him: You forgive me for what?
Me: Man, it's too much to talk about. Just know I forgive you.
Him: Okay, son.

From that moment on, I began to see my dad with eyes of compassion. I decided to let all the disappointments go. I started to think of him for the man he could be and not for what he had done in the past. It was one of the hardest things to do because, with my natural eyes, I saw a man who abandoned his family, gave up on his marriage, and never kept his word to his children.

However, around three years later after that conversation, my dad called me and told me he was sorry for all he had done. I was shocked. People who have seriously hurt others rarely come back and apologize, but he did it. After forgiving him years earlier, I finally heard the voice of the man I knew he could be. After that day, my dad and I talked more, and I never held the past against him. At times, I was tempted, but while talking with him, I could tell something was new, but I wasn't sure how the transformation occurred. But by that time, it did not matter. I was just excited that our relationship had greatly improved.

On October 29, 2008, my dad called me, and his voice was different. It was somber as if he had bad news. I remember that day because the Phillies won the World Series. After asking me how I was doing, he told me he had lung cancer and told me not to worry. I was somewhat in shock after hearing the news. As I held back my tears, I asked him how he was feeling, and he assured me that he felt pretty good. He told me that he was undergoing aggressive chemo treatments and that he would keep me updated.

PEOPLE SUCK, GOD IS GOOD

After we got off the phone, I had some hope. He did not give me many details, but I didn't ask many questions. A few months after that, we spoke again, and he told me that he had gone through many rounds of treatment. His voice didn't sound too encouraging, so I decided to visit him at the hospital in Southaven, Mississippi. When I arrived, he looked weak. As I looked at my father, I could tell he was fighting. But I could also tell he was tired. After hugging him and making sure the hospital was treating him okay, he asked me a question. It still brings tears to my eyes even as I write this:

> Dad: Son, do I have to be baptized to be saved?
> *Me: No, Dad. Who told you that?*
> Dad: This preacher told me that I have to be baptized to be saved.
> *Me: Baptism is just an outward declaration to the world of the salvation that has occurred inwardly by accepting Jesus Christ as Lord and Savior. Do you believe that?*
> Dad: Yes, that is what I thought, and I know that God will take care of me. If this is my cross to bear, I will gladly bear it.

As I sat there listening to my dad, I held back the tears. He was humble, thankful, and talked about bearing a cross. This is the man that I knew my father could be. That weekend with my dad may have been one of our best weekends together. As we sat and watched basketball with BBQ plates filled with ribs and chicken, I never once looked at him or treated him like a father who broke promises and never kept his word.

I never once brought up my mom and how he treated her. I never once brought up anything from the past because I had forgiven him and knew he was a new man. And as we were in the hospital room while looking at him lying in bed enjoying his food, I didn't see "that dad." I saw my dad, Malcolm Carl Walls Sr., as a brave man of God, staring death in the face with the confidence of entering into paradise. I saw a man who had willingly picked up his cross for the Lord and did not complain about his illness.

Sadly, not too long after that visit, my dad passed away. I am thankful that even with all the mistakes he made in life as a man, father, and husband, I was able to see him as the man I knew he could be. The vision I saw of him came to pass. I am thankful that God gave me a snapshot of the godly man my father had become. And in his last days, God showed me a man of valor and not a man of many flaws.

In Acts 10:9-16, Peter has an experience on a rooftop and gets a vision of something that would change the trajectory of his life. Take a look at the story.

> [9] The next day, as they were on their journey and approaching the city, Peter went up on the housetop about the sixth hour to pray. [10] And he became hungry and wanted something to eat, but while they were preparing it, he fell into a trance [11] and saw the heavens opened and something like a great sheet descending, being let down by its four corners upon the earth. [12] In it were all kinds of animals and reptiles and birds of the air. [13] And there came a voice to him: "Rise, Peter; kill and eat." [14] But Peter said, "By no means, Lord, for I have never eaten anything that is common or unclean." [15] And the voice came to him again a second time, "What God has made clean, do not call common." [16] This happened three times, and the thing was taken up at once to heaven.

For a moment, just imagine the scene. It was a nice day with perhaps a slight country breeze. Maybe the sun was shining, or it was a mix of sun and clouds. Maybe it was like Myrtle Beach in the fall. Either way, Peter decides to go to the rooftop for prayer.

While on the roof, he can feel the warm sun, and then he closes his eyes, thinks about the greatness of the Lord, and begins to pray. And out of nowhere, his stomach grumbles. He must have been praying hard. While he was waiting for lunch, his mind began to shift focus. He goes from thinking about his surroundings to a divine state of mind. Then, all of a sudden, the sky breaks, and he sees heaven open up.

He sees all kinds of animals, maybe even a possum (my interpretation). Now you know you are hungry when you have visions about possums. And the Lord tells him to kill and eat. With a scowl on his face, Peter is like, "No way, I am not putting anything uncommon or unclean in my body." Did we not just read that the Lord gave him a direct order, and he said, "NO, Lord, I can't associate with such things. I observe Your law." Peter rejected that which the Lord had provided. Peter missed it. He forgot what Jesus taught about in Mark 7:15:

> [15] There is nothing outside a person that by going into him can defile him, but the things that come out of a person are what defile him."

Jesus has already told them that what goes in the body does not defile them. So when Peter rejects the Lord's provision, in actuality, he is rebelling against the Lord. Yes, eating defiled food went against the Levitical law, but Peter missed the point of the vision. The theological thought is that the vision represented the entire world and how God was seeking to redeem all people and all nations, but Peter wasn't even thinking about that. The Lord then says to Peter, "Don't call unclean what I have made clean." And to get His point across, the Lord gave this vision to Peter not once but three times.

Anytime the Lord says or does something three times, we need to pay attention. Here is what happens next in Acts 10:

> [17] Now while Peter was inwardly perplexed as to what the vision that he had seen might mean, behold, the men who were sent by Cornelius, having made inquiry for Simon's house, stood at the gate [18] and called out to ask whether Simon who was called Peter was lodging there. [19] And while Peter was pondering the vision, the Spirit

said to him, "Behold, three men are looking for you. [20] Rise and go down and accompany them without hesitation,[c] for I have sent them." [21] And Peter went down to the men and said, "I am the one you are looking for. What is the reason for your coming?" [22] And they said, "Cornelius, a centurion, an upright and God-fearing man, who is well spoken of by the whole Jewish nation, was directed by a holy angel to send for you to come to his house and to hear what you have to say." [23] So he invited them in to be his guests.

Has God ever told you something that you did not receive on the first, second, third, or tenth time? Don't worry, Peter was the same way. He was perplexed by the vision, and as he was still trying to figure it out and connect the dots, there was a knock at the door. Three men were looking for him, and they told Peter that Cornelius, a Roman (non-Jew) who was an officer in the army, was looking for him. But this is no ordinary Roman officer. They told him that Cornelius, an upright, God-fearing man who was respected by the Jewish nation, was led by a holy angel to send for Peter to eat at his home.

Mind you, God had already told Peter these men were coming. Peter then invited the men inside. Ahhh...I believe Peter is now starting to get it. The vision is starting to become a reality. He is starting to see people the way God sees them. Warren Wiersbe once wrote: "The fact that Peter allowed the Gentiles to lodge with him is another indication that the walls were coming down."[55]

When was the last time you invited someone from a different walk of life to your home? You name it, not just ethnically diverse but different in lifestyle, sin struggle, sexual orientation, or medical condition. Too often, we get caught up in our homogeneous circles and avoid our neighbors. But when Peter invited these men into his home, the Jew-Gentile divide was starting to crumble. When you invite people you think are unclean into the sacred space of your home, you are making room for the walls of division to be broken down.

Here is how the story ends. The next day he rose and went away with them, and some of the brothers from Joppa accompanied him.

> [24] And on the following day they entered Caesarea. Cornelius was expecting them and had called together his relatives and close friends. [25] When Peter entered, Cornelius met him and fell down at his feet and worshiped him. [26] But Peter lifted him up, saying, "Stand up; I too am a man." [27] And as he talked with him, he went in and found many persons gathered. [28] And he said to them, "You yourselves know how unlawful it is for a Jew to associate with or to visit anyone of another nation, but God has shown me that I should not call any person common or unclean. [29] So when I was sent for, I came without objection. I ask then why you sent for me."

Peter and the men leave and go to the home of Cornelius. They ring the doorbell, and the door is opened. Peter walks in, and Cornelius is there with his family and friends. Cornelius then greets Peter by falling at his feet and worshiping him. Talk about showing a brother love. Indeed, this takes Peter by surprise. He tells Cornelius to get up.

Then he says (this is the Malcolm version), "Bruh...I am not supposed to associate with you people or anyone else who is not a Jew. But now I get it. I can't call you unclean. God has declared you are clean, and if God said it, that is good enough for me." Talk about a change of mind and heart. But let's read what Peter said in verses 34-35:

> [34] So Peter opened his mouth and said: "Truly I understand that God shows no partiality, [35] but in every nation anyone who fears him and does what is right is acceptable to him."

Peter gets it now. He sees the reality of the vision. God does not show partiality when it comes to who His children are. He does not treat those who come to him with a broken spirit and contrite heart unjustly, regardless of their background. Peter will never forget this vision. We know this because, in 1 Peter chapter 1, he writes:

> [22] Having purified your souls by your obedience to the truth for a sincere brotherly love, love one another earnestly from a pure heart, [23] since you have been born again, not of perishable seed but of imperishable, through the living and abiding word of God.

Peter is imploring us, after his experience, to love one another profoundly and sincerely from the heart. To look beyond their outward appearance and look beyond their past and culture and see them as a new person, a child of God, and perhaps someone who needs a second, third, or fourth chance.

How do you see people? Do you see them based on what they did 15 years ago or for who God wants them to be in the future? We get so caught up in past or current behaviors of others, and we look at them through tinted glasses, not even considering how God is shaping them. This is why so many people in the church wear masks, cover up their struggles, and put on the appearance that all is well.

This is indeed a tragedy because we are all rejects undeserving of God's grace. Outwardly, we are all messed up. But inwardly, a transformation is taking place. And as recipients of fantastic grace that is transforming us, how can we not extend that grace to others and look at them through a lens of love and look beyond their appearances or faults and see them the way God sees them? When we see people how God sees them, it is easier to forgive them. It is easier to love them. Think of 1 Corinthians 13:4-7 (NIV):

> [4] Love is patient, love is kind. It does not envy, it does not boast, it is not proud. [5] It does not dishonor others, it is not self-seeking, it is not easily angered, it keeps no record of wrongs. [6] Love does not delight in evil but rejoices with the truth. [7] It always protects, always trusts, always hopes, always perseveres.

Do you see it? Love is patient, which means it is deliberate and slow to judge. Love is kind, which means it is considerate. Love does not keep a record of wrongs, which means it does not maintain an account that it can review later. Do we love like this? Do we treat people like this? Do we see people the way God sees them? I love Peter's story because God confronts Peter's prejudice, bigotry, racism, elitism, you name it. God knew Peter's flaws, but in love, He also knew the man that Peter would become.

Before we go further, let's look at how God, through His love, saw people so that we can have a frame of reference for how we see people.

- Moses was a murderer, but God saw him as a deliverer of His people

- Abraham and Sarah doubted God, but God saw them as the parents of the promised child

- Rahab was a prostitute, but God saw her as a righteous woman

- Gideon was afraid, but God saw him as a mighty warrior

- David was an adulterer, but God saw him as a man after His own heart

Fill in your blank: You say or think you are a _____ but God sees you as _____.

God calls us to understand that no matter how sinful people are, they can be recipients of overwhelming, underserved grace. This is the victory of the Gospel of Jesus Christ. Maybe you think, "I have a hard time seeing people as God sees them." You are not the only one. And for those of us who do see people the way God sees them, we may not do it consistently.

In and of yourself, you can't do it. You can't see people like God sees them unless you begin to surrender your heart to Him. Author and church planter Anand Mahadevan wrote:

> Gospel transformation is often a slow process. It takes time because God doesn't merely fix our behavior. He changes us inside out. He brings about a heart transformation. This takes time. We often crush new followers of Jesus with the pressure of our unreasonable expectations. We naively assume that when someone becomes a follower of Jesus, all their sin patterns will vanish in a day. Not so. God works in us patiently, day-by-day, gradually, slowly, step by step. Remember one true and beautiful thing about grace. God will not forgive us without also transforming us.[56]

According to Ephesians 1, this is how God sees us, and this is the bare minimum of how we need to see each other. We are:

1. **Blessed** - We have **every spiritual blessing** in Christ Jesus (v.3). We have been made righteous in His sight and have resources, privilege, position, and power from God alone.
2. **Holy** - Because of the sacrifice of Christ, we are **set apart** and blameless in the eyes of God. (v.4)
3. **Family** - The follower of Jesus is in the **family** of God. We are unified under the Lordship of Jesus, and we are in a covenant relationship with God and each other regardless of our cultural background. (v.5)
4. **Forgiven** - Our sins have been **forgiven**. The worst things we have done. Christ died for that. (v.7)
5. **Recipients of His grace** - We deserve death, yet we have **unmerited favor** with God. (vv.7-8)
6. **Sealed** - Our future to spend eternity with God is secure because we have been **sealed with the Holy Spirit** (v.13)

This is our new identity as believers in the body of Christ. We have been created for a divine purpose. Part of that purpose is to love others in the body of Christ and healthily engage those who are different than us for the goal of oneness.

In 2017, I decided to cut the grass on a nice summer day. I got the lawnmower and pulled the cord to get started, but nothing happened. After many attempts, I decided to look at the troubleshooting section of the manufacturer's manual. After reading, I learned that the spark plug I had was too weak and dirty to ignite the fuel and air mixture in the carburetor. So I went and bought a new spark plug and exchanged it for the old one. When I swapped the old spark plug with the new spark plug, the lawnmower had the spark it needed so it could do what it was created to do.

Unfortunately, many Christians are using old spark plug thinking that is hindering them from doing what God created them to do and living the way God intends for them to live. Like the lawnmower, we have lost our divine spark. We continue to remain divided, and that is not what God has called us to do. We have to exchange how we look at people with the way God looks at people. We need to get our spark back to function the way God wants us to. Peter got the spark, and then something remarkable happened. Let's take a look at Acts 11:1-3.

> [1] Now the apostles and the brothers who were throughout Judea heard that the Gentiles also had received the word of God. [2] So when Peter went up to Jerusalem, the circumcision party criticized him, saying, [3] "You went to uncircumcised men and ate with them."

The news about Peter traveled fast, and his comrades were not too thrilled about his interaction with Cornelius. Here in the text, it is interesting that the men who criticized Peter were not upset about Cornelius' transformation but that Peter would associate with him. It's okay if he is God-fearing, but we don't associate with "those people." There will be naysayers when you decide to step up for true unity and peace. There will be people who will say, or at least think, "Why are those people coming into our church?" "Why is the pastor associating with that person?" "Why are they going to dinner with them?" why, why, why.... Let us not be surprised when people who are spiritually blind scrutinize us for seeing people the way God sees them and interacting with them. But it was this rebuke that led Peter to share about his transformation.

> [4] But Peter began and explained it to them in order: [5] "I was in the city of Joppa praying, and in a trance I saw a vision, something like a great sheet descending, being let down from heaven by its four corners, and it came down to me. [6] Looking at it closely, I observed animals and beasts of prey and reptiles and birds of the air. [7] And I heard a voice saying to me, 'Rise, Peter; kill and eat.' [8] But I said, 'By no means, Lord; for nothing common or unclean has ever entered my mouth.' [9] But the voice answered a second time from heaven, 'What God has made clean, do not call common.' [10] This happened three times, and all was drawn up again into heaven. [11] And behold, at that very moment three men arrived at the house in which we were, sent to me from Caesarea. [12] And the Spirit told me to go with them, making no distinction. These six brothers also accompanied me, and we entered the man's house. [13] And he told us how he had seen the angel stand in his house and say, 'Send to Joppa and bring Simon who is called Peter; [14] he will declare to you a message by which you will be saved, you and all your household.' [15] As I began to speak, the Holy Spirit fell on them just as on us at the beginning. [16] And I remembered the word of the Lord, how he said, 'John baptized with water, but you will be baptized with the Holy Spirit.' [17] If then God gave the same gift to them as he gave to us when we believed in the Lord Jesus Christ, who was I that I could stand in God's way?" [18] When they heard these things they fell silent. And they glorified God, saying, "Then to the Gentiles also God has granted repentance that leads to life."

As Peter tells the men about his transformation, he says something critical to the entire conversation. He said to them that the Holy Spirit fell on the men the same way it fell on them. But Peter did not stop there. He says that God has granted repentance that leads to life for the Gentiles. Peter is telling the men the game has changed. No more discrimination, no more exclusion, and no more ostracizing people based on their backgrounds or ethnicity. These Jewish believers have now been called to look at Gentiles as recipients of a new life in Christ.

It is refreshing to look at people from a positive, loving, and affirming perspective. When we look at people with the eyes of Christ and the attitude of Christ, it should give us more hope that God is still in the business of redeeming and renewing people the same way He saved and is renewing us. He is changing lives, and He wants us to see people not for who they are today but for who they will be in the future. Pursuing unity means also seeing people through the eyes of love and grace. Through forgiveness and redemption, God not only changes hearts but also perspectives.

My own experience with my father, Malcolm Carl Walls Sr, serves as a testament to this truth. Yes, he was a man of many failures, but I saw a man of great faith in his last days. It was through the lens of compassion that I was able to see this transformation. As we think about Peter and Cornelius, let us reflect on our own lives. Do we see people through a tainted lens of prejudice and judgment? Are we willing to change the old spark plugs of bias, hurt, and discrimination for new spark plugs of love, forgiveness, and compassion?

I pray that this chapter has encouraged you to examine your heart. Maybe, like me, you have to make a phone call and forgive someone.

10

All Words Matter

> *Set a guard, O Lord, over my mouth; keep watch over the door of my lips!* — **Psalm 141:3**

I spent most of my childhood in Greenville, Mississippi, also known as the River City or the Queen City of the Mississippi Delta. I recall growing up with my mom having a great commandment: Be in the house before the street lights come on. Upon this commandment hung every other rule in the household. The rule seemed strange to me because I had no idea what she meant. I was not sure if she wanted me in before it got dark because she was concerned for my well-being or if she wanted me to be in the house in time to wash up for dinner.

So, for most of my early to middle childhood, I had no idea what she meant, and I never dared to ask her because if I did, she would simply tell me, "Just do what I tell you to do." In my rebelliousness, I would sometimes cut it close and other times come in after the street lights came on. These infractions of the great commandment either led to an intense lecture or, more often than not, a whoopin'. In my adolescent years, I had come to learn that the "street light rule" was put in place to protect me. My mom wanted me to be in the house before dark because she was scared that I might get myself into some compromising situations or that someone would snatch me.

Growing up, I would hear rumors from friends and family telling me that when black folks go out at night, the Klu Klux Klan (KKK) would kidnap them, take them down by the riverside, kill them, and dump them in the river. This is probably why my mom wanted to protect me, but she never explained it. She only said, "Be in the house before the street lights come on." I believe my mom assumed I fully knew what she meant by the rule.

She became a victim of the false consensus effect, which is the belief that one's personal beliefs, views, thoughts, values, actions, and language are relatively understood by everyone. Because of my mom's authority over me and my fear of being whooped, I never asked her to explain her great commandment; I simply agreed with it and continued with my life. I never knew that I was potentially putting my life on the line the numerous times I rebelled.

Meaning Makes the Difference

Sometimes, after preaching, I encounter people who approach me with encouraging words. "Good word, pastor," or "Man, you were preaching today." Other times, I have people approach me who want to educate me on what I should have said or considered saying when preaching. On one occasion, one of my Christian brothers came and told me that he liked the sermon one Sunday. He then went on a rant about the Black Lives Matter movement and how it is a Marxist movement.

The irony is that I never mentioned or said anything remotely close to Black Lives Matter in the sermon, yet he felt the need to tell me about their beliefs in the conversation. Once he paused, I asked him, "Are we talking about Black Lives Matter, the organization, or the phrase?" This was my attempt to slay the FCE. He responded, "I don't think the organization represents the truth." My response then was, "Well, what is truth?" He looked at me puzzled, then talked about how he wanted them to be truthful and that President Trump was doing a great job.

He never answered my original question about Black Lives Matter, which kept me in the dark about what he was trying to communicate. He assumed that I knew exactly what he was talking about or that his thinking was the standard way of thinking for everyone. After finishing, I gave him the traditional "God bless you, bro" and walked away. Unfortunately, even with my probing questions, the FCE was still alive, bringing me no further enlightenment after the conversation.

Too often, in discussions around sociology, politics, gender, or life in general, we often say certain things with the assumption that the listener fully understands what we are talking about. We go on our rants, gauge where people are, and get consumed with getting our points across to convince people of our ideologies. We often use terms like "evangelical," "black lives matter," "all lives matter," "white privilege," "defund police," "toxic masculinity," and "#MeToo," believing that everyone has the same definition. That is the gist of the False Consensus Effect.

We don't all share the same definitions of the words and phrases we use because we live in divided spaces. The meaning of a word in one space may be different in another. Dr. Samuel Proctor once wrote, "Our country is polarized terribly on matters of diversity and intercultural relations."[57] The America we live in has unique cultural and subcultural lifestyles, languages, and meanings. And because of these uniquenesses, it can be complicated to have everyone understand and agree on the terms or phrases we use.

The way we view life is different. Our experiences are different. Therefore, it is normal for people to talk about issues of injustice, women's rights, and religion differently. We use words and phrases that may mean one thing to us, but it means something different to the hearer. Let's start by looking at a word and a phrase that can have varying definitions. The definitions below are my own, based on various conversations I have had.

Word	Meaning 1	Meaning 2	Meaning 3
Privilege	Advantages that anyone can have if they work hard enough or achieve a measure of success.	Unearned advantages that tend to benefit white people.	Advantages that have been historically passed down that influence systems to oppress minorities.
Black Lives Matter	The organization	A phrase to express the desire to end the senseless deaths of African Americans that could have been avoided.	The desire to see African Americans in power and conquer white Americans and white oppression.

Simply based on the terms just listed, communication without full explanation can lead to confrontation and further separation. The words we choose as we pursue unity have to be defined so everyone in the conversation knows precisely what is being talked about. If not, the listener will default to separation out of frustration, have a fear of being labeled because they used a different definition, see things differently, feel ignored, or leave the conversation angry. Of these potential outcomes, separating from people is the quickest resolution for most.

It is also the easiest because it is a natural reaction, and if we are separated, we don't have to deal with the discomfort of the conversation ever again. As humans, in our sinfulness, we desire to take the road with the least amount of suffering. And because of this, we dare not lean naturally into discomfort. It is easier to segregate and perhaps the most preferred method of operating. We do not take the time to talk to one another or listen to one another, yet we are implored to be quick to listen and slow to speak (James 1:19).

To listen is to understand, and to understand is to ask questions, and consider what is being said. In the listening phase, we will be uncomfortable. It is absurd to think that conversations about injustice, diversity, or equality will give us a warm and fuzzy feeling. We will always approach it with a level of unease, especially when we are around people from different cultures.

It is vital to remember that as we converse with people, the goal is not to win but to love and dwell in unity. If our goal is to win, we will not demonstrate the patience needed to listen and have meaningful dialogue. If our goal is to win, we will inevitably lose patience with people, which is the opposite of what love does.

The brother who came to me after the sermon to share his thoughts about Black Lives Matter emailed me a few days later and thanked me for sharing my point of view. I did not want to make him feel like he was wrong, nor did I want to dismiss his thoughts or beliefs. I just wanted him to think about what he said and consider how his words could be misunderstood depending on whom he was engaging in conversation with. Jesus practiced this perfectly, even at an early age.

His parents were looking for him, and the Bible says, "After three days, they found him in the temple, sitting among the teachers, listening to them and asking them questions." There is no recording of Jesus arguing with the religious leaders. It appears as though he was seeking to question them about what they believed and practiced. For disciples of Jesus, the goal should always be unity, and being unified means listening and asking questions. This process should lead us and others to the truth. It also helps to provide clarity.

Creating unity is not about persuading the other person to adopt a different ideology, getting them to feel a sense of guilt about history, or claiming or reinforcing a position of superiority. Unity is only created by having open and honest dialogue, asking questions, listening, and saying what we truly mean so that everyone walks away looking a little more like Jesus. The framing of any good relationship is the language we use in communication. Just like a house needs framing so that a home can be built properly, relationships require an excellent communication framework that consists of well-defined language to create unity.

Douglas Sharp said, "Language is not merely a means of communication in and about the world in which we live. It has a way of shaping that world as well as being shaped by it."[58] But using good language in communication is never easy because we always say things that can be hurtful. James 3:8 says, "but no human being can tame the tongue. It is a restless evil, full of deadly poison." As we share our hearts, there must be grace given by the listener.

As our language is unpacked to get to the real meaning of our words, our relationships can go to the next level. And the deeper the relationship goes, the more uncomfortable it will be. Conversations with clear and good language genuinely glorify the Lord. But how is that? One of the side effects of the FCE is that it makes one overconfident and even condescending. But when we start to unpack terms and phrases, consider what others think, and have honest conversations, we slowly gain humility, and that is where the Lord wants us. Psalm 25:9 says, "He leads the humble in what is right, and teaches the humble his way."

To achieve this, there must be at least two things: 1) A mutual understanding of the words and phrases we use as we communicate with each other, and 2) Using language that is kingdom-oriented. Let's journey through some other words that can often have different meanings in conversations. Below is another list that has been created to spark additional thoughts as you have conversations with people.

Word	Meaning 1	Meaning 2	Meaning 3
Terrorist	Those who are radical Muslims who want to destroy Western culture.	Anyone (foreign or domestic) who uses physical violence to intimidate others.	Any person who creates an environment of fear to change the political status quo.
Racism	The savage physical mistreatment of individuals based solely on skin color.	When the majority group allows their prejudice to influence their power and privilege to marginalize or oppress minority groups physically or systemically.	When one people group uses negative behavior or course language with the sole intent to make fun of or mock other people groups.
Abortion	Having the personal right to voluntarily end a pregnancy without societal or legal repercussions.	Taking away opportunities from anyone at any stage or condition of life, so that they will not have a meaningful life.	A medical procedure that should never occur regardless of the circumstances.

Illegal Alien	Persons from another country who are considered newcomers who contribute to society and are undocumented.	Persons from another country that are deemed as a security threat to America and American culture.	Persons from another country who are unlearned, inferior to Americans, and should be treated as such.
Gender	The idea of being either male or female based on genitalia.	How a person self-identifies based on various characteristics and experiences.	A social construct that can change over time and from one culture to another.
Christian	A person who has a relationship with Jesus Christ by grace through faith.	An individual who practices portions of the faith because of culture or upbringing.	Those who practice syncretism by combining Christianity with other religions, politics, and/or Western culture

Again, the concise definitions in the previous table above are based on conversations I've had with others. As we analyze the meanings of the words we use, we realize that there can be differences in definitions. By reading the definitions, it is easy to see how conversations about a single topic can go astray. For believers in Christ having these conversations, the goal is to walk away looking more like Jesus. If this is the goal, then God's Word must be the authority that brings closure because as we read the Bible, we must conform our lives to what it says.

This is another cause of discomfort. Because when we use the Bible as our guide for conversations, our humanity will always conflict with God's divinity. We may realize that our definitions are more secular than Biblical, the narratives we give people are unfair, and the labels we place on people are plain sinful. If we are going to be unified, then we need to stop trampling over one another with our words and start using kingdom language with one another for the sake of unity. Kingdom language represents truth, and truth always precedes unity.

Kingdom Language

In the summer of 1991, my mom decided to go back to school and pursue a career in nursing. Her decision led us to relocate from Greenville, MS, to Greensboro, NC. In Greensboro, we moved into a nice apartment complex with many families, but I usually kept to myself since I was new to the area. Once I started going to high school, I started meeting other teenagers. Most of them laughed at my deep southern accent. And even though it hurt to hear them mocking me, I did not say anything because I wanted friends. My mom was a respiratory therapist at the time, and she would often work double shifts and on weekends. So when I came home from school, I had no social interaction because she was at work. I was the typical latchkey kid.

One day after school, tired of being alone, I went outside and looked for anyone to hang out with at my apartment complex. While walking around, I saw a white kid just roaming around doing nothing. As I recall, I hesitantly walked up to him and asked him if he wanted to hang out. He said, "Sure!" and like typical teenage boys, our hanging out slowly but surely became a competition. The apartment complex surrounded a small lake, so we took turns seeing who was best at skipping rocks on the water. After that, we decided to race.

We created a starting line, and then after a three-count, we took off. I dusted that kid and took pride in beating him. As a black kid who grew up in Mississippi, I always cherished the moments when I beat or was better at something than my white counterparts. So this victory,

PEOPLE SUCK, GOD IS GOOD

in my mind, was my way of getting revenge for 400 years of slavery. I was talking so much trash and dared him to race me again. At this moment, he yelled, "Shut up nigger." After his explosion, I thought it was best to meet his aggression with aggression. I remember violently cussing and lunging at him. With a loud expression of words and the threat of violence, he ran away. I was alone again; however, I was proud of standing up for myself. I continued walking outside by the lake, and after about 15 minutes, a police car rolled up.

A white officer got out and said something to the effect of, "Son, I have to talk to you." He took me to the apartment complex gym and said, "I heard you fought with another boy." I responded, "No, sir. He called me a 'nigger,' and I cussed him out." He looked at me sternly and said, "Son, you are going to be called a "nigger" a lot more, so you need to get used to it. If I have to come back, I will take you to jail." After that, he left, and I was in the gym of my apartment complex crying because the one that swore to serve and protect me not only abdicated his responsibility as an officer he also used language that reinforced a white supremacist ideology.

He was essentially telling me that I should accept being called a "nigger" for the rest of my life. After that altercation, I never told my mom or anyone else what happened to me that day. All I could do was ponder the question in my head, "Will I be a nigger for the rest of my life?" In that conversation, the officer did not lean into my hurt and seek to understand what happened. His goal wasn't to get to the truth. He lacked charity and any sense of servanthood. He simply reinforced the language and racist views of the other kid.

As I got older and reflected on that moment, I realized that being called a nigger was not the greatest evil. The greatest evil was how the white officer attempted to get me to buy into a term and ideology that made me inferior to white people. Words can be insidious and can take up residence in the deepest part of our souls. In addition, the words we use and live by tend to reflect who we are and what we worship. I wonder what my life would have been like if I had adopted an inferior identity based on the officer's word and not the identity I have in Christ based on God's word. I also have wondered how many other people's lives reflected this disastrous terminology and ideology after being told they were inferior or just objects.

Words are powerful and can change the trajectory of someone's life. Proverbs 18:21 says, "Death and life are in the power of the tongue," and because oneness is a huge undertaking, we cannot interact with each other as the officer interacted with me. As brothers and sisters in Christ, we need to lean into each other's pain, and we must rely on the supernatural power of the Holy Spirit to overcome this divisive stronghold in the church. There is no cookie-cutter program, law, or economic package that will fix the disunity that exists in the church.

One of our greatest weapons is the sword of the Spirit, which is the word of God. Using the Word of God and kingdom-focused terminology in conversation with those in the body of Christ may seem foreign because we only tend to use it for our enemies or in spiritual warfare. And many in the church do not see division as spiritual warfare. But indeed it is, and all of us in the body of Christ must have a divine and gospel-centered posture that leads us to use apt words at the right time so that we represent the Kingdom of God with everyone we come into contact with.

In 2018, after Hurricane Maria, I had the opportunity to visit the town of Utuado in Puerto Rico. Once I landed in San Juan, I began to see the devastation of the hurricane. Once we got to Utuado, those who lived there were still without power. This truly bothered me, and when I got back, I shared my experience at church. After I spoke, one of my Christian brothers, who is white, came to me and said, "Do you know how much white people have done for Puerto Rico? America has done a lot for them." After listening to him, I asked him if he wanted to go to lunch later that week. He agreed, and we met up a few days later.

I intentionally wanted to revisit the conversation, so I told him that he implied that America equals white people. But that America is not a white nation; instead, it is a colorful nation. I shared with him how

I grew up in the South, went to college like many others, worked in corporate America, and answered the call to ministry. I wanted him to see that the two of us were not significantly different. I told him that I wanted to get to know him because we are brothers in Christ. He then shared about himself and how he grew up. Before we finished lunch, he apologized for what he said.

There was love and forgiveness extended before we went our separate ways that day. I do believe we both walked away from that lunch mutually edified. If communication is the framework of any good relationship, then we can't shy away from having tough conversations. Tom Holladay once wrote, "Words are like bricks-you can use them to smash a window, or you can use them to build a foundation."[59] We must begin to use kingdom language with kingdom definitions as defined or governed by the Bible for the betterment of each other.

Too often, we use secular jargon that is emotionally or experientially driven in conversations to resolve spiritual issues. Frequently, these words do not promote unity and kingdom outcomes, which directly contradicts the Lord's prayer of oneness in John 17. Because secular language is so divisive, we must abandon those definitions, redeem the terms, and begin to use kingdom language and definitions that are driven by God's agenda. The next table below has some examples.

Word	Kingdom Meaning
Intercultural	Embracing our God-given differences and leveraging those differences to advance the kingdom of God

Equality	The state of being image bearers of God, equal heirs, and partakers of the same promises in Christ through the gospel.
Equity	When someone within the body of Christ helps create equal environments for others so that they have the opportunity to be successful and glorify God.
Justice	Showing the love of God by being good stewards of people, honorably caring for the meek, being merciful to the poor, loving our neighbors, seeking peace, and sharing resources while simultaneously making decisions that are ethical and just.
Community	Being entirely accepted by those who share the common thought and belief that Jesus died and rose again, we have the same eternal destination, we have the same commandment to love God and others, we have the same loyalty and allegiance to God, and the same goal which is to glorify God and make disciples.
Abortion	Taking away the God-given life, future greatness, or kingdom opportunities of anyone at any stage of life.

Due to the infestation of secularism and syncretism in the church, we must examine our language and definitions and hold them under the microscope of biblical truth. The Word of God governs the words in the table previously listed. Our responsibility is that we must be convinced that kingdom language based on and found in the Word of God is and will be a salve to the soul. The use of kingdom language locks us in to share the truth of both what is and what can be by God's grace.

When we use kingdom language, we begin to change the world and put chaos in order. Kingdom language acts as a divine bridge that brings God's people together as one with God and each other. The more we use it, the more we confront the darkness and illuminate hearts to see the light of the King, His will and humbly submit to Him. Our dedication to God's Word and using language that reflects His kingdom is non-negotiable. As children whom the Father has adopted, we should use language that is more communal and that chops down the tree of ego that exists in all of us. Chopping like this means we willingly make ourselves uncomfortable for true unification. And when we use language that nurtures others, we will begin to eradicate the endemic division in the church and the world.

11

One Sound, One Heart

> *So we, though many, are one body in Christ, and individually members one of another.* — **Romans 12:5**

In high school, I was a trombone player in the band. I remember the band director always emphasized the importance of playing in tune and not trying to outplay one another. For her, every instrument was necessary, had value, and had its notes to play. Though it is small, the flute is as important as the tuba. The trumpet was just as crucial as the saxophone. I took this to heart and made it my mission as a trombone player to always play in tune and never let my desire to be heard risk the unified sound of the band. One of my favorite moments of playing the trombone was being a part of the marching band during football games.

I loved marching on the football field during home games because of the energy from the crowd. The band would line up to go out to the field, and the drummers would always lead because they set the tone for the excitement. As the drummers played, the energy through the entire band grew. As we rocked back and forth, with heads nodding, we started marching in place. I could feel the vibrations from the drums in my body. Once the drum major blew the whistle and gave the signal, we would march towards the field as a group. We were so in step with one another as we marched.

On one particular occasion, as we marched to the field, I could tell that my pants were a little loose, but with all of my excitement to play, I didn't tighten them up and assumed everything would be fine. As we were on the field playing, it was great. As a band, we were rocking it. But as we kept marching and going from formation to formation, I could feel my pants loosening up more and more. As we shifted to the next position on the field, coming to the end of the song, I ended in a front-line position where everyone in the stadium could see me. While I was standing in a stationary position, playing my heart out, my pants came down. I could hear gasps from onlookers, which quickly turned into laughter.

It was an embarrassing moment, but all I could think about was how much I didn't want to mess up the sound. So what did I do? I kept on playing. Despite the gasps and comments from the stands, I continued to play that trombone with all of my heart. During one of the most embarrassing moments of my life, I did not want to mess up the unity of the band's sound. As soon as there was a pause in the music, I pulled my pants up so that I could continue marching. To this day, one of my best friends will not let me forget about that moment and swears there is a recording of what happened. In the end, I was proud of myself because I believed in the importance of the band having oneness of sound even at the expense of being embarrassed.

The dilemma in the universal church is that many people are playing out of tune or trying to outplay one another. In one church, you will hear only the tune of the social dilemmas of the day and political leaders being vilified. In another church, you will hear the tune about the spiritual depravity of humanity and that his most profound need is Jesus, who has atoned for his sin while the social struggles of people are dismissed. And in another church, you will hear the tune about social justice and not man's need for a savior. And to make matters worse, the aforementioned tunes are trying to outplay each other.

It is mission critical that the church plays the same song at the same tune, albeit with different notes, and be on one accord in orthodoxy (doctrine) and orthopraxy (the correct practice of doctrine). We must proclaim the tune of biblical justice while declaring how it is a part of the gospel. We need to have the tune of social commentary about the world and how we, as believers in Christ, need to address it from a gospel perspective. We also need the tune of our need for a savior and our communal responsibility, which is also within the gospel. All of these need to be proclaimed, through word and deed, in harmony with the other.

The church as a whole should not proclaim one louder than the other. If we can proclaim our message and live it out as one, the power of the gospel will be demonstrated astronomically. However, this only happens when we preach all of scripture, deny ourselves the desire to be applauded by people, and are more concerned with glorifying God. By emptying ourselves of self-love and disregarding what others will think of us, we can produce a unified sound that rings out the pure Gospel of Jesus and live out the oneness we are called to, both in spirit and in practice.

The book of Ephesians offers a blueprint of the oneness that we have as believers and how that should be lived out. We learn that Apostle Paul is encouraged by their faith and love for one another within its pages. The Ephesian church understood that a relationship with Jesus was not just about salvation but also impacted every aspect of their lives. Some say that the believers in Ephesus believed in the idea of "my life for your life" in the way they loved each other and lived each day.

This letter written by Paul was not just for the church in Ephesus but for all churches. In it, we read a message of spiritual oneness for all believers and practical oneness for the church despite the cultural differences among the people. Another way of saying it is that the Apostle Paul encouraged them to be one, live as one, go out and reach others, and glorify the Lord.

Spiritual Oneness

Ephesians 2:1-3 says:

> [1] And you were dead in the trespasses and sins [2] in which you once walked, following the course of this world, following the prince of the power of the air, the spirit that is now at work in the sons of disobedience— [3] among whom we all once lived in the passions of our flesh, carrying out the desires of the body and the mind, and were by nature children of wrath, like the rest of mankind.

This is the human condition without Jesus. At one point in time, all of us were spiritually lifeless and hopeless. We were disciples of the world, living in selfish "independence" as we walked in darkness. The Apostle Paul reminds us that we all have missed the mark of God's righteousness. We were all spiritually dead in the flesh and have fallen short of God's glory. We have allowed popularity, power, and politics to guide us. We have permitted individualism and the American dream to define us. We have allowed the way we look to define our identity.

We all have a longing for significance, we all desire to be adored, all of us want to excel, we all want to influence the lives of others, we all crave attention, we all want to feel important, we all want to be recognized. This drives one group or person to think they are superior to another. That is one of the most significant lies of the enemy, and without Christ, this is the human condition before God's grace stepped in to redeem us. Ephesians 2:4-7 states:

> [4] But God, being rich in mercy, because of the great love with which he loved us, [5] even when we were dead in our trespasses, made us alive together with Christ—by grace you have been saved— [6] and raised us up with him and seated us with him in the heavenly places in Christ Jesus, [7] so that in the coming ages he might show the immeasurable riches of his grace in kindness toward us in Christ Jesus.

Through Christ, because of our new identity in him, we have experienced newfound freedom and life. We are God's masterpieces. Whether you like it or not, God has taken some messed up, oppressive, wicked, abused, and hurt people and has renewed them spiritually and shaped them to be more like Jesus. Therefore, when we look at one another, we should see people who used to be utterly hopeless and selfish but whom God is transforming into faithful servants who reflect the image of Christ. Spiritually, we were all once bound for hell together. We were the villains and victims of sin. And now, we, through Christ, are bound for heaven together.

Once we recognize that as followers of Jesus, we were all spiritually broken and shared the same Christless eternity, we can now rejoice that we are chosen recipients of God's grace. And as recipients of the grace, we are a part of God's ultimate plan, which is to unify all things in Christ. Ephesians 1:9-10 says:

> [9] making known to us the mystery of his will, according to his purpose, which he set forth in Christ [10] as a plan for the fullness of time, to unite all things in him, things in heaven and things on earth .

The Apostle Paul is telling the believers in Ephesus that God's end goal is to unify everything under the Lordship of Christ. That is ultimate peace. The question that remains is," Why would this speak to the people's hearts in Ephesus?"

Like major cities today, Ephesus was a multiethnic/multicultural center of trade with diverse moral beliefs, worship of false gods, and different socioeconomic groups. Therefore, it would make sense that the church would be composed of multiethnic believers who were rich, poor, and coming out of some form of idol worship. The natural implication is that there would have been people who may have thought that they were economically or spiritually superior to someone else. But the Apostle Paul reminded them that since God chose them, they are now equals, and God is uniting them all under the authority of Christ.

For us today, it means that no matter what or who you used to worship, what sin you have committed, how rich or poor you are, or your cultural background, Christ is now your authority, and you are in God's family by God's choice. Talk about a morale booster! If your life has been characterized by sin, the worship of false gods, wealth, or poverty, it is incredible to know that God still chose you. His love is extended to all and is effectual for those who receive Jesus for the end result of oneness in Christ.

Like those in the Ephesian church, all of us, as followers of Jesus, are now unified under the Lordship of Christ, having a new identity. We are in a covenant relationship with the Father. We have been redeemed from spiritual poverty and have a unique spiritual family for eternity. And because of the mercy of God, all of us who call Jesus our Lord and Savior must realize that we are spiritually one with other people who do not look, act, or think like us. As believers in Christ, we share one blood, one faith, one baptism, and one Lord. And though we all have mess in our lives, we have all been forgiven, we are all recipients of His grace, and we have all been sealed with the same Holy Spirit.

Practical Oneness

As long as we live in this world, we will be tempted to focus only on the spiritual aspects of the faith, which are profitable but require little to no investment in the lives of others. We must flee the temptation to only converse about embracing people different than us. By embracing, I mean recognizing the differences and leveraging them for deeper relationships. Conversations are beneficial, but if we limit our actions to mere talk, we will never showcase the power of the gospel. We must humble our attitudes to God and be fervent about intentionally practicing, outwardly, the oneness that we have spiritually in the body of Christ.

The greatest application of practically living out oneness is recognizing that we all have the same mission. We all want to make God known to the world and make disciples. Part of this is done by those in the body of Christ demonstrating true love for one another. John 13:35 says, "By this all people will know that you are my disciples, if you have love for one another." When I look at other sheep who now follow the Great Shepherd, I must realize that they are no different from me and that we are called to serve together and love one another.

We must all be in harmony in word and deed as a church, albeit sometimes uncomfortable. We must abandon the belief that we serve in silos or have different agendas and recognize that our mission as the church is to participate with God in the holistic transformation of people for the world's redemption. God delights in us as we move as one and influence the world for His glory. Jeremiah 9:23-24 states:

> [23] Thus says the Lord: "Let not the wise man boast in his wisdom, let not the mighty man boast in his might, let not the rich man boast in his riches, [24] but let him who boasts boast in this, that he understands and knows me, that I am the Lord who practices steadfast love, justice, and righteousness in the earth. For in these things I delight, declares the Lord."

God is not calling us to have ego trips and remain selfish as we wait for the return of Jesus. As we devote our lives to Christ, we should be dedicated to covenant works. It is the work of conversing, connecting, and collaborating with others.

Conversing - Intentionally meet with others

We cannot just tolerate people and believe that we are honoring God. We must intentionally seek to engage with people who are different from us. We need to seek people out, meet with them, and begin a journey of listening to them and embracing their stories, history, culture, values, and struggles. Listening does the following: 1) Builds trust 2) Forms relationships 3) Enables learning 4) Allows for hearing and understanding.

These moments can be very uncomfortable because there may be a clash of values, or our worldviews may be different. Or we may interpret things the wrong way. The problem is that we never really listen to each other and often misunderstand what is being said. So we have to alleviate those misunderstandings by asking probing questions like "What do you mean by that?" or "Can you unpack that a little more so I can understand?" This is where there needs to be grace given on both sides to seek a common understanding as we talk to each other.

Connecting - Find Common Ground

As you share stories, culture, values, etc., listen to one another and look for commonalities in your journeys. Finding common ground helps you move from "I" to "We." This means we are getting closer to each other. So I am decreasing the distance between us. Finding common ground will help you make relational deposits in the other person's life. You may find opportunities to affirm their dignity or help restore it. You may find opportunities to celebrate their victories. You may find opportunities to challenge one another to be better in a particular area. You may even find that you all have similar hurts and can heal together.

Collaborating - Willingly surrender

John Maxwell once said, "you have to give up to go up."[60] It is surrendering self to the bigger picture of unity. The idea of surrender here is to surrender doing things my way and genuinely accepting and implementing new ideas that others have. It is surrendering my opinion and empowering others to speak up. It may be a surrender of some authority. It may be that you will see that the person who is different from you may be better equipped to do something that you usually would do. At this point, you are no longer focused on yourself. Instead, you are focused on a shared mission and focused on the team. In the surrender phase, it is no longer about your personal preferences. The goal is empowerment, creating oneness, taking the glass ceiling off of people, and allowing them to thrive.

Try It

You may have had some bad experiences in your life, but the truth is that God wants to use those experiences for the betterment of others. The work of conversing leads to connecting, and connecting leads us to collaborating with our neighbor. This is a surrendering of personal preference for the sake of the gospel. As we move forward as believers, let us remember that our diversity is our strength. What happened to me on the football field was a moment where my discomfort became an act of unity.

Sometimes, we will have to endure pain or maybe even embarrassing moments to see the unity we are striving to achieve. As we continue in our journey of faith, let us remember that all of us are beautiful instruments that God is using. He wants us to get out on the field that is called the world and play in such harmony that people will be in awe. As beacons of hope in Christ, we are called to be the ultimate band, where the glorious sound of the gospel is ringing out for all to hear in epic proportions.

12

God is Good: An Invitation

> *Blessed are the peacemakers, for they shall be called sons of God* — **Matthew 5:9**

You are finally at the end, and I hope that God has been speaking to you about how to come to the end of yourself and has helped you to see that we all have our levels of brokenness. The longer I live, the phrase "people suck" becomes more clear... I am the people! Despite my mistakes, I recognize God's grace and the call He has for us to live as one and be better. This is why we must die to ourselves daily.

When I think of unity, I just want to think of going to church or leading a Bible study with like-minded believers. I don't want to love or associate with people who are different from me or, I think, do not deserve to be loved. I don't want to wash the feet of the person who will betray me, and I don't want to eat dinner with the folks who will abandon me. But on my journey, I have learned that to be better, even with the potential of being hurt, is a part of the cost. I have also learned that if we are going to be peacemakers and build toward unity, God invites us to four things. The first is an invitation to service.

SERVICE

In Acts in chapter 9, Saul has an encounter with Christ. As he is going through his transformation and conversion, he is blinded by the Lord.

While he is blind, the Lord has a conversation with another person named Ananias. I encourage you to read this story for yourself, but here is my modern-day translation:

> *The Lord: Ananias, I got something for you to do. I need you to go to Straight Street.*

> Ananias: Not a problem. I can do that.

> *The Lord: Look for a man of Tarsus.*

> Ananias: No problem. Say less.

> *The Lord: Look for a man named Saul.*

> Ananias: Wait...who? Come on...Really?

It was all good until the Lord mentioned Saul's name. Ananias was willing, but his fear of Saul made him hesitant. Now, his fear is real – Saul had a history of violence towards Christians. If it were anyone else, Ananias would have probably jumped at the opportunity to serve. But he does not want to help this guy because he fears for his life. Ananias tells the Lord what he has heard about Saul as if God does not know his history. We can be like Ananias. We can be willing but hesitant. There are some people we want to serve, and there are other people we don't want to serve because they make us feel uncomfortable.

I can relate to Ananias. There have been times when God has called me to serve, and my response was, "Lord, I know you told me to go, but what if...?" "What if I get hurt?" "What if I get sick?" "What if I lose everything?" "What if I can't take care of my family?" When it comes to being called to serve, the biggest killer of the calling is "what if." And after the what-if moment, I make the situation worse by catastrophizing or making these doom-and-gloom scenarios that will probably never happen. When I catastrophize, I am now at the place of forgetting that God is sovereign.

I have learned that I should not have all the what-ifs or catastrophize the call from God because no matter what happens, my future is secure in Him, and I succeed. The invitation to pursue unity with others will only result in success. If they persecute me, I win. If they come to know Jesus Christ as Lord and Savior, I win. If they reject me, I win. If I lose everything for the sake of Christ, I win. If I have to take a pay cut, I win. If I die, I win. Why? Because God is sovereign.

God holds all the power and knows the future, and He can handle future threats and circumstances that come against me. The same goes for you. When you accept the invitation to pursue unity with others, you must hold firmly to the knowledge of the sovereignty of God. He is in control, and He gives us hope that is stronger than our what-ifs. The future calling means we have to serve the least, the lost, and the left out. We must serve those that we fear, those that we think are suspect, the people that get on our nerves, and those we try to avoid.

SUFFERING

Acts chapters 6 and 7 describe the story of a man named Stephen. He was filled with grace, wisdom, faith, power, and the Holy Spirit. I'll let you read these passages on your own, but basically, he was taken by the religious leaders because of some trumped-up charges, and he had to deal with their nonsense. (My translation, of course.) When he was asked about these accusations, he preached a sermon. He spoke the truth. In Acts chapter 7, Stephen calls these religious leaders mean, stubborn, heathens, and deaf to the truth.

He tells them that they betrayed and murdered Jesus, the Messiah, and have deliberately disobeyed God's law. Stephen went in on these cats! He called them out. Sometimes, this is what you have to do. But like Stephen, we do it by proclaiming biblical truth. They ended up stoning Stephen as he called out, "Lord Jesus, receive my spirit." And falling to his knees he cried out with a loud voice, "Lord, do not hold this sin against them." And when he had said this, he fell asleep." (Acts 7:59-60).

Stephen was wrongly accused, lied on, and suffered for the sake of the gospel. Often, the proclamation of biblical truth precedes godly suffering. Notice I said the proclamation of biblical truth. Not human opinion. Not political beliefs. Not secular ideologies or sociological theories. If unity is going to exist, people need God's truth, not our opinions or feelings. The invitation to pursue unity is an invitation to being at peace with the call to suffer. You'll notice that Stephen does not want to hurt those who are hurting him.

Why? Because the message of biblical truth for unity must be given without hostility. A brother of mine, Don Amaker, who has gone home to be with the Lord, once said, "If you want to know how a man lives, watch how he dies." Stephen suffered and died proclaiming the truth. We, too, are called to proclaim truth even while suffering.

STEADFASTNESS

If we are to fulfill the call to build unity, we must focus on a kingdom vision of what will be and not what is. This invitation implores us to keep fighting the good fight of faith and having hope for what will be. Hebrews chapter 12 encourages us to look to Jesus as the perfect example of faith. He did not give up. With all his suffering, Jesus knew that resurrection was coming. He endured the cross, absorbing all the pain because he knew something greater was coming. He knew there was about to be a homecoming in heaven.

For us, the call is to be steadfast and keep our eyes on heaven above and not on earth below. God has given us everything we need to live a godly life. As you endeavor to pursue unity with others, I want to encourage you to stay on track. Too often, when adversity hits, we lose sight of the Kingdom. Our fears, doubts, and discouragement get in the way. God is calling you to come to the end of yourself for the sake of someone else, but you can't do it if you are not focused on the kingdom.

I get it. I know they hurt you. They are different from you. You don't like them. You think they are stupid. They think you are just a victim of some circumstance in life. Or maybe you've been trying to pursue unity with others, and it seems like nothing is turning around. Don't become discouraged or distracted, and don't give up. Keep your eyes on Jesus. There is nothing wrong with being discouraged; it is wrong to *stay* discouraged. Sometimes, being steadfast means you have to take a break. And when you do it, don't look at your imperfections; look at the perfection of Jesus!

SUCCESS

During the 1997 NBA championships, Michael Jordan played game 5 against the Utah Jazz despite flu-like symptoms. He initially struggled but managed to score 17 points in the second quarter before facing more difficulties in the third. However, he persevered and scored seven points in the fourth, leading his team to victory. He didn't start perfectly, but he served his team despite how he felt. He suffered for his team. And even though he looked tired and was physically sick, he kept on. He was steadfast because he was focused on success.

God is looking for disciples who are willing to serve on His team regardless of how they started in life or how they feel. It doesn't matter if you are afraid or if you feel inadequate. He is looking for folks who are willing to suffer while serving. And he is looking for people to be steadfast. He wants people who have their eyes on the Kingdom because that is the final prize.

God wants you to make a difference, so persevere through it all (mistakes, anxiety, discouragement, doubt, impatience, hurt... all of it) and do it because of the confident hope we have in Christ and the future hope that the Gospel brings. As we navigate through life, we inevitably realize that God is good, but people...not so much. And in God's goodness, He wants us to be better in order to pursue unity with all people. And we must have a high level of determination to do it.

ONE LAST WORD

As you prepare to close this book, I encourage you to carry on the work of shattering the walls that divide and building toward unity with others. As you have been reading, I pray that you have learned what I learned along my journey. That is, you have the power to:

- Let go of the old life and embrace the new life God has given you.
- Focus on the truth of God's word and let it guide you.
- Overcome all obstacles because God is with you on this journey.
- Pursue and cultivate relationships with people who are different from you, even when it feels uncomfortable.

Achieving unity is not easy. It is not a concept; it is a calling. It requires us to serve when we don't want to. Suffer when we don't have to. And remain steadfast when we want to give up. But just like Jordan, we must press on to secure success.

This is a divine invitation. It's an invitation to serve when you are hesitant. It's an invitation to suffer for truth. It's an invitation to be steadfast and not get discouraged by the challenges you will face. And ultimately, it's an invitation to be successful and see the goodness of God on full display. The unity journey can seem impossible. But let me ask you one last question. How would you live if you knew that God is the God of the impossible? My journey is a testimony that He is God of the impossible and He will be God of the impossible for you. He is calling us to trust in His power, trust in His victory, and be better as we relate to one another.

Keep your eyes on the Kingdom, knowing that Christ has already secured the ultimate success. And because He wins, we win!

ACKNOWLEDGEMENTS

I want to thank Patsy, Bob, Samantha, Joe, Cherly, Ed, Tricia, and Alfreda, my mom. You all invested in me to make this book happen. Thanks for believing in me and how God has called me to be a peacemaker in the church.

Many thanks to David Olshine for encouraging me to write. I remember our initial conversation over lunch at CIU. Your insight was invaluable. You have been in my corner since day one, and you kept me accountable to get it done.

I want to thank SMS Ministries Publishing and the team for the hard work put into editing the book. You all, indeed, saw the best in me and pushed me to have my voice heard.

To the readers of the book, J.H. Kim, Connie Edwards, and Ed Norris. Thank you for providing honest feedback and making sure the book honored God and remained authentically me.

I also want to thank Pastor Jeff, the staff, and the congregation at Sandhills Community Church. You are my family, and I am blessed to be a part of an intentionally diverse church that seeks to lead all people to live Christ-centered lives. My time serving at Sandhills has been rich, and I look forward to serving there for many years to come.

Lastly, to everyone I have encountered, who is different than me. Thank you for your perspectives on life and your willingness to share your life with me. I cherish each of those moments and how they have been foundational in my desire to pursue unity with all people.

ABOUT THE AUTHOR

Dr. Malcolm Walls, Jr

Dr. Malcolm Walls, Jr. and his fantastic wife have three children: Imani, Malcolm III, and Alexander. They currently reside in Columbia, SC. Dr. Walls graduated from North Carolina A&T State University with a degree in Marketing. He earned his Master of Divinity and Doctorate of Ministry degrees from Biblical Theological Seminary. In 2017, Dr. Malcolm Walls became the Pastor of Outreach and Next Steps at Sandhills Community Church.

Dr. Malcolm currently serves as an adjunct professor at Columbia International University, teaching Multicultural leadership. He has been blessed to serve as an elder, youth pastor, and executive pastor in different church contexts, which has given him invaluable experience. Serving in outreach has allowed Dr. Walls to engage with other local, regional, national, and global churches and ministries. He has successfully built strong connections with para-church ministries and Christian non-profits, and has been a guest speaker at their events.

REFERENCES

[1] Dane Ortlund, Gentle and Lowly (Wheaton Illinois, Crossway, 2020) pg 114
[2] Warren Wiersbe (The Wiersbe Bible Commentary. The Complete New Testament (Colorado Springs, CO. David C. Cook) pg. 927
[3] John MacArthur (The MacArthur Bible Commentary. (Nashville, Tennessee, Thomas Nelson pg 1922)
[4] Mark Deymaz, Building a Healthy Multi-Ethnic Church, Josey-Bass. San Francisco, CA pg. 22
[5] Wagner, Larry. Help Me Help Others: Practical Ways to Build Healthy Relationships. Redemption Press. Enumclaw, WA 98022 pg. 44
[6] Rom. 8:29 NLT
[7] Wagner, Larry. Help Me Help Others: Practical Ways to Build Healthy Relationships. Redemption Press. Enumclaw, WA 98022 pg. 50
[8] King, Martin Luther. A Testament of Hope: The Essential Writings and Speeches of Martin Luther King Jr. HarperCollins, New York, NY. pg 245
[9] Tozer, A. W, "Attributes of God," 104.
[10] John Calvin. The Institutes of Christian Religion. Presbyterian Board of Publication and Sabbath-School Work. Chapter 1, pg 37
[11] Koyama, Kosuke: Three Mile an Hour God. SCM Press Ltd. London
[12] Raymond C. Ortlund Jr. Preaching the Word Commentary: Isaiah - God Saves Sinners. Crossway, Wheaton, ILL pg. 76
[13] Gunter, Nate. Me Monster: The selfish boy who learns to love. TGJS Publishing. United States
[14] The Spiritual Combat. Fr. Dom Lorenzo Scupoli. Pg. 7
[15] King, Martin Luther, The Measure of a Man, Fortress Press, 1959, Minneapolis, MN, pg 9
[16] Bunyan, The Works of John Bunyan: Experimental, doctrinal, and practical. Pg. 197
[17] Dane Ortlund, Gentle and Lowly: The Heart of Christ for Sinners and Sufferers (Wheaton, Il: Crossway, 2020), 93
[18] Martyn Lloyd-Jones, Seeking the Face of God: Nine Reflections on the Psalms

REFERENCES

(Wheaton, Il: Crossway, 2005), 34

[19] Spencer Perkins and Chris Rice. More than equals Racial Healing for the sake of the Gospel. InterVarsity Press. Downers Grove, IL page 104

[20] Mark Vroegop. Weep With Me: How Lament Opens A Door For Racial Reconciliation.
Crossway, Wheaton ILL. Pg. 37

[21] Fenelon, Francois. The Seeking Heart. Christian Book Publishing House. United States of America. Pg. 69

[22] Cedar, Paul A. The Preacher's Commentary. James, 1, 2 Peter, Jude. Thomas Nelson Publishers, Nashville, TN. James 4:1-3

[23] Priolo, Lou. Selfishness. From Loving yourself to loving your neighbor. P &R Publishing. New Jersey. Pg 15

[24] Goff, Bob. (2019, May 1-3). Orange Conference: Everybody Always [Conference Presentation]. Atlanta, Ga. United States.

[25] Dr. Tony Evans. Oneness Embraced: Through the Eyes of Tony Evans: A fresh look at Reconciliation, The Kingdom, And Justice. Moody Publishers, Chicago. Pg 27

[26] Tom Holladay. The Relationship Principals of Jesus. Zondervan. Grand Rapids, MI pg. 13

[27] Dr. John Perkins. One Blood: Parting Words to the Church on Race and Love. Moody Publishers, Chicago ILL. Pg 100

[28] Luke 23:34 CSB

[29] Wiersbe, Warren. The Wiersbe Commentary Nehemiah 1. Page 754

[30] A Biblical Answer for Racial Unity Kress Biblical Resources. Woodlands, TX. Pg. 25

[31] R. Kent Hughes. Preaching Commentary: Romans. Crossway, Wheaton IL pg. 206-207

[32] Dr. Martin Luther King Jr. Strength to Love 1963. p 37

[33] Timothy Keller, The Meaning of Marriage: Facing the Complexities of Commitment
with the Wisdom of God

[34] Preaching the Word Commentary, 1-3 John. Chapter 5. Pages 74,75,80,82

[35] Deymaz, Mark, Building a Healthy Multiethnic Church, Jossey-Bass, San Francisco, Ca. Page 85

[36] Ken Camp, Segregated Churches Lack Credibility In Diverse Society. https://www.baptiststandard.com/news/texas/segregated-churches-lackcredibility-in-diverse-society-deymaz-said/ October 14, 2018, Baptist Standard

[37] Schaeffer, Francis. How Then Should We Live?: The Rise and Decline of Western Thought and Culture (New York: Fleming H. Revell Co., 1976)

[38] Piper, John, What is Christian Unity?, DesiringGod.org, https://www.desiringgod.org/articles/what-is-christian-unity

REFERENCES

[39] So to Speak' podcast: How Daryl Davis, a black man, defeats the Ku Klux Klan with open dialogue. Podcast March 9, 2017 by Nico Perrino

[40] A.W. Tozer. The Crucified Life: How to live out a Deeper Christian Experience. Bethany House Publishers. Bloomington, Minnesota pg 17

[41] Rice, Chris and Perkins, Spencer. More than Equals, Intervarsity Press, Downers Grove, IL., Page 33

[42] William Barclay's Daily Study Bible, Acts 2

[43] Thabiti Anyabwile. Christ-Centered Exposition: Exalting Jesus in Luke. B&H Publishing, Nashville, TN pg. 64

[44] Keller, Tim Life in the Gospel. A Biblical Critique of Secular Justice and Critical Theory", https://quarterly.gospelinlife.com/a-biblical-critique-of-secularjustice-and-critical-theory/

[45] Hughes, R. Kent. Preaching Commentary Acts 2. Page 49.

[46] Piper, John, What is Christian Unity?, DesiringGod.org, https://www.desiringgod.org/articles/what-is-christian-unity

[47] Allen David L. Preaching the Word Commentary: 1-3 John, Fellowship in God's Family. Crossway, Wheaton ILL. .page 151-152

[48] Tozer, A.W. The Attributes of God. Vol. 1. Wing Spread Publishers, Camp Hill, PA page 95

[49] Fenelon, Francois The Seeking Heart, The Seed Sowers Christian Publishing House. Sargent, GA page 146

[50] Jones, Noel. Let it Go. https://www.youtube.com/watch?v=WxVn1bODnEQ

[51] Lloyd-Jones, Martin. Children of God Vol. 3, Life in Christ: Studies in 1 John. pp 107-118 (sermon "Love in Action")

[52] Perkins, John. Dream With Me: Race, Love, and the Struggle We Must Win. Baker Book, Grand Rapids Michigan. Pg. 137

[53] Manton, Thomas. A Treatise of Self-Denial, Chapel Library, Pensacola, FL pg. 8

[54] Lewis, C.S. The Chronicles of Narnia. Book 1: The Magician's Nephew. Harper Troph. New York, NY. pg 75

[55] Wiersbe, Warren W, The Wiersbe Bible Commentary. Acts 10 David C Cook, Colorado Springs, Co pg. 356

[56] Mahadevan, Anand. Grace of God and Flaws of Men. LIfeway India Publishing pg 38

[57] Proctor, Dewitt Samuel and Gardner C. Taylor. We Have This Ministry: The Heart of the Pastor's Vocation. Judson Press, Valley Forge, PA page 22

[58] Douglas R. Sharp. No Partiality: The Idolatry of Race & The New Humanity. Downers Grove, IL, Intervarsity Press. Pg 30

[59] Holladay, Tom. The Relationship Principles Of Jesus, Zondervan. Grand Rapids, MI Page 189

REFERENCES

[60] Maxwell, John. The 21 Irrefutable Laws of Leadership. HarperCollins Leadership. Pg 185

www.ingramcontent.com/pod-product-compliance
Lightning Source LLC
Chambersburg PA
CBHW072158070526
44585CB00015B/1192